Iowa's Wild Places

Iowa's Wild Places

An Exploration with

CARL KURTZ

IOWA STATE UNIVERSTIY PRESS
AND THE
IOWA NATURAL HERITAGE FOUNDATION

CARL KURTZ, master photographer, naturalist, and prairie
reconstructionist, has a B.S. in fisheries and wildlife biology
from Iowa State University. He taught natural history
photography at Iowa State for 14 years and has conducted
photography workshops throughout Iowa. He also has
taught several adult education courses on nature photography and has presented more than 500 lectures to students
and civic groups.

About 650 of Carl's photographs and 20 of his articles
have been published in 50 different regional and national
publications, including books, magazines, and calendars.
His work has also appeared in advertising, cards, posters,
and museum displays.

Carl and his wife, Linda, live on a farm near
St. Anthony in western Marshall County in central Iowa.

© 1996 Iowa State University Press, Ames, Iowa 50014
All rights reserved

Book and jacket design by Kathy J. Walker

Printed and bound in Hong Kong

First edition, 1996

Kurtz, Carl
    Iowa's wild places: an exploration with Carl Kurtz.—1st
ed.
    p.   cm.
    Includes bibliographical references (p.   ) and index.
    ISBN 0-8138-2161-4
    1. Natural history—Iowa—Pictorial works. 2. Nature
photography—Iowa. 3. Landscape photography—Iowa.
I. Title.
QH105.I8K87   1996
508.777—dc20   96-2422

To Linda
Who made this book possible

Contents

Foreword

One early February morning a glint of red caught my eye from outside the kitchen window. I looked again. Most definitely a speck of red gleamed in the morning sunlight off the crust of snow covering the front lawn. I moved slightly and there was another, and another—this one green, others blue and gold. The lawn danced with tiny colored lights. The night's frost had left ice crystal prisms on the snow's surface that split the first low rays of the sun into colors of the rainbow and created a moment of magic that I had never before witnessed. I wondered: How often does this happen? What special weather conditions caused it? Who else had noticed? One person would know. If anyone had marveled over this gift of nature, perhaps capturing it in words or in a photograph, that person would be Carl Kurtz.

I've known Carl for nearly 25 years; his photographs have graced our living room walls for the same period. Most Iowans with any interest in natural history know Carl and, for not a few, that interest has been nurtured through the window of Carl's photography. Haven't we all sighed and asked, Why don't my pictures turn out like this? The answer is in this book.

That special quality in Carl's photographs isn't produced by special equipment: Carl's cameras, as he explains, are relatively simple. Neither is it derived from a professional knowledge of photographic methods, although this is undoubtedly a prerequisite to assuring that the subject is faithfully portrayed in its photographic image. The *special something* of Carl's photographs comes from Carl's eye and from his intimate knowledge of his subjects, be they birds or flowers, rolling storm clouds or a snow-capped seed head nodding in a winter storm.

In our photography most of us succeed in capturing images; Carl captures processes. We capture the snow cap; Carl captures the storm. Through this book we begin to understand the difference.

There is another message in Carl's photographs and in his vivid descriptions of nature's inhabitants and their world: We are losing something precious not only in the physical disappearance of natural areas but also in our inability or unwillingness to set aside time for appreciating our natural world. In our daily rush, we don't take time to watch a woolly worm climb a flower stalk or to count the petals on a black-eyed Susan. And if we do, we feel guilty for "wasting" our time or someone else's. What a shame! Shouldn't such moments of quiet contemplation be part of the good life we work so hard to obtain? If we recognize no place for time unrelated to product and profit, what do we gain? These are thoughts brought to focus in reading this book. They are distressing thoughts and wistful thoughts, and they are mixed with thoughts of gratefulness for wild places and for the images and experiences Carl shares with us.

Iowa's Wild Places is not a catalog of the birds of Iowa or the plants of Iowa or the geological regions of Iowa. It is an opportunity to experience Iowa through the eyes of a gifted observer—to see and understand the intricate patterns of the rare and the common, the immense and the tiny, the dramatic and the subtle expressions of nature in our home state. Most of us cannot hope to match Carl Kurtz's exquisite interpretations of nature through lens and word. This is no cause for lament but all the more reason to appreciate Carl's talents and his gift to us in the pages of this book.

DONALD R. FARRAR
Department of Botany
Iowa State University

Preface

For more than 20 years I have contemplated a book about Iowa's natural landscapes. A fascination with nature began early in my life, and as a naturalist I have tried to arouse that curiosity in others. Only when we begin to understand the workings of the universe do we see the value of all life forms. Only through the protection of biological diversity and prudent use of all resources will humankind survive.

I owe an enormous debt of gratitude to numerous individuals who have directly or indirectly assisted me through the years. Dick Baker, Jim Dinsmore, Donald Duvick, Diana Horton, Dennis and Karlene Kingery, Roger Knudson, Connie Mutel, John Pleasants, Lois Tiffany, Dean Roosa, Sylvan Runkel, and Nancy Slife reviewed manuscripts or parts of essays for technical accuracy. Their time and energy, constructive comments, and suggestions are sincerely appreciated. Jean Prior and Don Farrar deserve special recognition for reading most chapters for scientific accuracy.

Countless individuals across Iowa have assisted me during the photographic process that has consumed nearly half of my life. They provided ideas, sites, directions, vehicles, food, shelter, and companionship. Each photograph has a list of individuals who indirectly made it possible. Larry and Margaret Stone have been invaluable in my exploration of northeastern Iowa. Roger Landers, professor of botany at Iowa State University until the late 1970s, graciously took me on forays to all parts of the state over a six- or seven-year period looking at natural areas in the course of his tree-ring research. It was with his constant assistance that I was able to develop an understanding of ecological processes. My color printer and friend, Bill Burt, not only gave encouragement but also reconstructed the colors in one older transparency, a time-consuming and difficult job.

My adventures in Iowa might not have happened had my parents not permitted me to find my way in the world without becoming trapped in the eight-to-five business workday routine. A flexible time schedule is absolutely critical if one is to experience and photograph nature's best displays.

Work on this project with Bill Silag and the staff at Iowa State University Press has been a pleasure. Bill gave me encouragement and ideas while keeping the time frame flexible.

I am deeply grateful to the Iowa Natural Heritage Foundation for funding the color portion of this book. Mark Ackelson and Anita O'Gara have been a constant source of support during the past 15 years.

Finally, this book would not have become a reality were it not for my wife, Linda. She has accompanied me on nearly every excursion during the past 12 years and has provided input at every level.

Iowa's Wild Places

Our time on the earth is like an eclipse—

we too are just a passing shadow

in earth's history.

May our lives be a legacy

of good stewardship for those

who follow.

Eastern cottonwood leaf melted into lake ice along the sandy north shore of Storm Lake, Buena Vista County.

The Art of Seeing

*E*ach day is a new creation. Events we see today will never again be experienced at the same place because the natural world is constantly changing. As time passes natural systems diversify and take on different characteristics and forms. Individual species—whether plant or animal—may come and go, but the biological system that nourishes life is constantly renewed.

Learning to see takes practice and perseverance. Many opportunities, adventures, and discoveries are missed because our vision is impaired. Whether in the backyard or the wilderness, we see what we expect to see. The observer with preconceived ideas often fails to find satisfactory results.

Seeing is an act of curious observation. It is more than just opening our eyes—the clutter and debris of everyday problems must be cleared from our minds. We need to approach the world with child-like openness and enthusiasm. Children greet each day with a sense of discovery as they take in the world around them. A few individuals retain these child-like qualities throughout life, but most working adults suppress these attitudes with the pressing demands of everyday life. At retirement many individuals slow down and readjust the pace of their lives. With a new sense of awareness,

Winter prairie with Indian grass and the last remains of a snow cover at the Marietta Sand Prairie State Preserve, Marshall County.

they begin to apply the experiences of a lifetime to the world around them.

High-speed travel on modern freeways leads many individuals away from good observation. In the rush to reach a destination, travel time becomes a necessity which must be endured. Only dramatic events such as storms make an impression, and should they impede our progress, it may be a negative one. When the mind becomes focused on a future place and time, one cannot enjoy the present.

A new view of the world around us often begins with bird watching. Since birds come to us, we are soon aware of common birds that inhabit or pass through our backyard. Since all life forms are connected, the quest to see new birds may lead us to search for wildflowers, observe clouds, identify insects, or collect rocks.

Some individuals learn to see by taking photographs. By isolating a part of the world within the camera's viewfinder, they learn to see and think in terms of shape, texture, line, and color. In the search for subjects, photographers find new ways of viewing the ordinary and familiar.

Photographers must rekindle in others this sense of discovery as they convey the world around them. The camera has no creative powers of its own. It is simply a light-tight box with a lens on one end and light-sensitive film on the other. What the photographer sees, the camera records.

Great photographs are made with care, perseverance, and planning. The photographer must have knowledge of the subject and the type of light which best accents its form. Although different types of film may record the scene quite differently, the greatest variables are light quantity and quality. Low light from the rising sun is often warm and soft and can be used to emphasize texture and form. Midday sunlight is strong and harsh and causes great contrast between sunlight and shade. Soft diffused light when there is fog or mist may give the scene a feeling of mood and depth. Precise timing can determine success or failure. The photographer

Blue flag iris and fallen leaves along the edge of a prairie pothole marsh at Anderson Lake, Hamilton County.

may also incorporate symmetry, rhythm, and alternation in the design.

Seeing takes time, practice, and experience. It requires spiritual and emotional involvement as well as physical effort. Seeing helps us to grow as individuals and to find enjoyment wherever we are. Our knowledge of geology, roadside plant communities, wildlife, the region's agriculture, and the culture of the people that inhabit the land richly enhances life. Life becomes part of a total experience—we are not simply onlookers. The artist Frederick Franch sums it up best: "It is not the pursuit of happiness, it is stopping the pursuit and experiencing the happiness of being [wholly] there."

*Brook lobelia, grass-of-parnassus, and slender gerardia in a calcareous
fen at Silver Lake Fen State Preserve, Dickinson County.*

Diversity

T he human mind tends to lump together the strange and
    unfamiliar. Because our senses are overwhelmed by new
    circumstances, we need time to sort things out. This basic
human trait is often a problem when it comes to land preservation.
A large segment of our population sees a woods as only a stand of
trees, a prairie as a grassland quite similar to most pastures, and
marshes as wetlands which produce mosquitoes and ducks but
otherwise have little value. Most people feel one natural area is
essentially as good as another unless it has high scenic value.

To naturalists, however, subtle differences exist in natural
communities even though they may be just across the road from
one another. While scientific criteria are used to evaluate many natural areas, scientists are not the sole providers for the protection
and management of all natural areas. The Nature Conservancy's
Iowa Registry program lists some 900 sites in private ownership—a
total of 35,000 acres. While these private landowners are aware that
their areas have value in a natural state and are concerned about its
future management, frequently they know little about their "great
possessions."

Iowa is blessed with many natural areas, although more than

90 percent of the state is under intensive cultivation. Some tracts are large—perhaps several thousand acres or more—but most are between 10 and 200 acres, and some are minute—a quarter of an acre or less. The largest and best-known areas have been studied extensively, but little is known about the majority of them.

Natural areas within Iowa's borders collectively contain an amazing variety of plants and animals. Some species occur statewide; others exist only as small remnant populations. Each species occupies a specific place, or "niche." Unlike plants, animals may move about in response to weather and food supplies. Although plants are anchored in soil, they may be nearly as elusive as animals because they are apparent only during certain seasons. Woody plants such as trees are obvious exceptions to the great majority of herbaceous plants which die back to the ground each year or overwinter as seeds.

Surveys of Iowa's native plants and animals reveal nearly 1,600 native plants (including 76 tree species), 120 species of butterflies, 136 species of fish, 370 species of birds (150 of which nest within the confines of the state), and 66 species of mammals. Not only have many plant and animal species been found in new locations in recent years, but scientists have also discovered one species new to science. The prairie moonwort, a small fern, was discovered in the Loess Hills in 1982.

All components of living systems fall into one of three categories. At the base of the food chain is the "soil," with water, minerals, and a multitude of decomposers (microorganisms such as bacteria, molds, and fungi) which break down wastes such as grass, leaves, feathers, and bones into organic material so they can be recycled.

"Producers" are the green plants which use water, minerals, and carbon dioxide as raw materials, absorb and store sunlight through a process called photosynthesis, and give off oxygen while producing carbohydrates. This liberation of oxygen keeps the supply in the atmosphere constant and makes life possible. Plants also produce fats; in peanuts and sunflowers the fats are stored in seeds. From carbohydrates plus minerals such as nitrates and phosphates, plants form amino acids and proteins, which become the building blocks of life.

"Consumers" are the animals (like us) who eat green plants or eat other animals which eat green plants. This process passes energy on to higher levels, although it is not all transferred at each step. Some energy is lost when it is given off as heat. Thus the activities of humans and all other animals result in a loss of energy, while green plants alone build up the supply of energy.

At all levels, organisms are interrelated and dependent upon one another. Yet we often fail to see that we too are part of the web and that without a multitude of other plants and animals, we cannot survive. Although the system is simple in many ways, the links between each level form a complex network.

In many parts of the world, natural areas are either being lost entirely or are in some way degraded by human encroachment. This usually means that some or all species which occupy those areas are either lost or displaced. When this happens, the community has fewer species of plants and animals, or in biological terms, less species diversity. For example, a prairie that is plowed and turned into a cornfield may be reduced from 300 self-sustaining species to one which is not self-sustaining. Some birds and small mammals may continue to use the area, but most will be displaced. This is not to say that we should replant all of our cornfields to native grasses and flowers for the sake of diversity. However, because existing natural areas serve as benchmarks, saving them is a wise investment in the future. They are indexes of original soil quality as well as biological reservoirs of Iowa's past.

Plants and animals also exhibit another form of diversity known as genetic diversity, or variation within a species. In the human species we recognize each person's uniqueness. Some individuals are tall, some short; some have long arms, others short fingers.

Red oak, alternate-leaf dogwood, maidenhair fern, and interrupted fern on a north-facing slope in sugar maple–basswood forest along Wexford Creek, Allamakee County.

Natural hair and skin color may vary from light to dark to shades of red. This is genetic diversity in humans. We may not be able to see genetic diversity as easily in plants and animals, but its existence is critical for the health of a population of monarch butterflies, sedge wrens, or white oaks.

Biologists who study a specific population of animals for an extended period of time eventually recognize their subjects as individuals. Over the years we have kept many deer mice in captivity. At first they look essentially the same, but we soon see subtle differences in their coloration and that they have very different personalities. The same can be said of bison and bumblebees.

Species diversity in a natural community provides community stability and protection from invaders, such as disturbance or disease. Genetic diversity may also protect individuals from disease. We are familiar with Dutch elm disease, where a fungus carried by a bark beetle caused the death of most old American elms in the 1970s. If the gene which made elms susceptible had been present in only a small portion of the population, we would still have old American elms today.

If genetic diversity for resistance or tolerance to pests or to environmental stress is present within a species, traits which assure the survival of a species are often selected; thus populations of individuals have a better chance of adapting to environmental change. We recognize that the person who has many interests and hobbies is sometimes better able to cope with change than the person who has few or none. In natural systems, as in individuals, diversity produces strength and uniqueness.

Natural systems do not deplete themselves or the land. Soils become richer and more productive as the diversity of plants and animals which utilizes them increases. Civilizations which destroy the diversity of plants and animals that bind and nourish the soil eventually collapse. They have undermined the very foundation upon which they stand.

Crustose lichen–covered Precambrian-age Sioux quartzite with circular colonies of the moss Grimmia *surrounding the mosses* Hedwigia *and* Tortula, *rock spike-moss, and the lichen* Cladonia *at Gitchie Manitou State Preserve, Lyon County.*

Bedrock Outcrops

Outcrops of bedrock form a very small but important aspect of Iowa's landscape. In most cases, they have been exposed by eons of water erosion at a rate which is almost imperceptible in a human lifetime. These surface features are a unique part of Iowa's landscape since, in most places, the subsurface bedrock is mantled by glacial till and windblown loess.

The oldest exposed bedrock is Sioux quartzite, found only at Gitchie Manitou State Preserve in Lyon County in the very northwest corner of Iowa. The west border of the preserve is the Big Sioux River, and the north border is South Dakota. On the geologic timetable, it is called Precambrian and is nearly 1.7 billion years of age. The composition of this light-reddish stone is quartz sand grains cemented with silica. Sioux quartzite is nearly impossible to scratch with a knife, but the abrading action of wind and weather over time has polished some surfaces to a glass-like finish, while other outcrops show grooves etched by glacial ice.

Microclimates exist on the surface and in small depressions and cracks in the Sioux quartzite. My first experience at Gitchie Manitou came in the oppressive heat of summer when the soft yellow flowers of brittle cactus and demure magenta blossoms of flameflower were prime. These are but two of a host of species which make the rugged landscape their home. Multicolored crustose lichens create a mosaic on the surface of many exposures which gives the hostile environment a special charm even on a cold midwinter morning. On some rock faces, mosses of the genera *Grimmia*, *Hedwigia*, and *Tortula* grow in mixtures and form circular clumps or small hummocks. *Grimmia* and *Hedwigia* are somewhat specialized, occurring only on acidic rock surfaces such as the quartzite. Tallgrass species such as big and little bluestem, slough grass, and side-oats grama occur on this prairie remnant as well as buffalo grass. In a sense, Sioux quartzite is Iowa's headstone, its age more than a quarter of earth's history.

Sandstone outcrops are young in comparison to quartzite, and exposures occur in many river and stream valleys throughout the state. Geological outcrops in central Iowa are about 300 million years old and belong to the Pennsylvanian geologic period. My favorite places to see sandstone in sharp relief are at Ledges State Park in Boone County, at Dolliver State Park and Woodman Hollow in Webster County, along the Iowa River between Steamboat Rock and Eldora in Hardin County, and at Wildcat Den State Park in Muscatine County. Each is unique, yet they share many similar characteristics.

Sandstone is porous and able to hold water like a sponge. Thus a host of bryophytes and pteridophytes—that is, mosses and ferns—find sandstone a perfect substrate to grow on. Many species need a consistent moisture supply, especially in the hot, dry weather of summer. Where sandstone exposures are shaded or north-facing, common polypody, walking ferns, spinulose shield fern, and marginal shield fern often grow directly on the sandstone surface. Shining club moss, broom moss, hair-cap moss, and cedar moss, which has fern-like leaves, may be present on loose sandstone talus, stabilizing fragile erosive slopes. I have also often found wild columbine and sharp-lobed hepatica growing on vertical sandstone

Walking ferns on moss- and lichen-covered Pennsylvanian-age sandstone blocks at Wildcat Den State Park, Muscatine County.

surfaces with mosses, lichens, liverworts, and ferns.

The action of moving water easily carves sandstone, forming small waterfalls and chutes in deep ravines. Two readily accessible sandstone outcrops are along Pease Creek at Ledges State Park and in Boneyard Hollow at Dolliver State Park. At the Lower Ledges one can wander along the creek, which continues to erode away the sandstone, creating habitats for mosses, ferns, and wildflowers. In the spring it is especially delightful when there is new green on the sycamores and redbuds are in blossom.

Sandstone outcrops also occur in northeast Iowa. St. Peter sandstone formations are 440 to 515 million years of age and from the Ordovician geologic period. Along the Mississippi River, a readily accessible example of this group underlies the surface dolomite at Sand Cave in Pikes Peak State Park.

South of the park, the river bluffs are deeply dissected with small streams flowing through shaded ravines which descend toward the river or to interconnecting streams. Late one autumn, outdoor writer Larry Stone and I explored the steep slopes to find sluiceways connecting quiet pools in moss-covered sandstone. A local farmer told us about finding his missing cow stranded between two sheer ledges in a steep-sided ravine. The cow was weak from a lack of food and had to be fed on location for some time before it could be led from this natural corral.

Even older Cambrian-age Jordan sandstones, 515 to 530 million years of age, also occur in northeast Iowa. The best example is easily seen next to the Great River Road between McGregor and Marquette.

Most limestone and dolomite formations are in eastern Iowa, especially in the bedrock-dominated northeast called the Paleozoic Plateau. These carbonate rocks were deposited undersea during the Silurian and Ordovician geologic periods, about 420 to 475 million years ago. Some limestones are called dolomites, which means magnesium-bearing rock.

Broom moss, cedar moss, and northern red oak leaves on loose Pennsylvanian-age sandstone along the Iowa River at Fallen Rock State Preserve, Hardin County.

Some of the best examples of limestone outcroppings occur along the Silurian Escarpment, the front edge of a geologic formation that underlies Brush Creek Canyon State Preserve in Fayette County; Backbone State Park in Delaware County; Retz Memorial Forest, Bixby and Mossy Glen State Preserves in Clayton County; and White Pine Hollow State Preserve in Dubuque County. At White Pine Hollow, constant water erosion along meandering Pine Hollow Creek, a tributary of the Little Turkey River, has created the rugged landscape. Steep bluffs with precipitous cliffs, talus-covered slopes, caverns, outcroppings on every hillside, and huge broken blocks lying scattered along the creek bottom make hiking difficult. In the midst of old exposures, fresh fractures provide ample evidence that the geological process continues today.

Along many streams and rivers in the northeast, one can find large blocks of limestone which have broken away from the exposed bedrock surface and fallen or slid downslope. No area has a more dramatic example of this phenomenon than Bixby State Preserve, where blocks as large as small houses are lying in general disarray over the entire slope. These limestone outcrops are shaded by an overstory of trees. In early May we can find a wide variety of mosses and ferns, such as bulblet bladder fern, fragile fern, and maidenhair fern, mixed with yellow violets, rue anemone, wild ginger, and dutchman's breeches. Some slopes also have Canada yew, a short evergreen shrub which can form a dense ground cover. It is often browsed extensively if the slope is accessible to deer. On limestone surfaces exposed to the drying effects of sunlight and wind, one may find the smooth cliff-brake fern. It is characterized by small, fine, bluish leaves and frequently is tucked into an eroded opening on a vertical surface.

Other parks which feature prominent limestone or dolomite formations include Maquoketa Caves State Park in Jackson County, Palisades-Kepler State Park and Dows State Preserve in Linn County, and Starr's Cave State Preserve in Des Moines County. The dramatic

Water-sculptured Mississippian-age limestone on Rock Run Creek near the Iowa River in Rock Run Canyon, Hardin County.

Old eastern redcedar atop Ordovician-age dolomite palisades north of Bluffton on the Upper Iowa River, Winneshiek County.

limestone overhangs along Flint Creek which contain Starr's Cave belong to the Mississippian geologic period and are about 325 million years of age, nearly 100 million years younger than those outcrops of the Silurian period in northeast Iowa. Old American sycamore trees line Flint Creek; their white trunks with gray, greenish, and brown mottling make this a very attractive site. Beneath one of the overhangs, a small hanging garden of mosses grows on a sheer vertical surface where water seeps through the limestone.

In many places along the Upper Iowa and the Yellow rivers, high, exposed limestone and dolomite walls make river access difficult. These rocks were formed during the Ordovician period, about 450 million years ago. Old redcedars and eastern white pines often crown blufftops and ridges; they grow in shallow soil or over the rock surfaces by sending roots into cracks and crevasses for water, nutrients, and support. Balsam firs occur on the steep northeast-facing slopes at the Bluffton Fir Stand State Preserve northwest of Decorah along the Upper Iowa River and on similar slopes at Mountain Maple Hollow along the Yellow River in southwest Allamakee County. The balsams, with their pointed spires, are mixed with white pines that have pagoda-shaped crowns, yellow birches (which are rare in Iowa), and paper birches with white trunks that stand out best after the leaves have fallen.

In the understory of this cool, moist environment one can find a great variety of bryophytes. One of my favorite mosses is tree moss, which can cover entire rock surfaces like a dark green shag carpet. It can be mixed with a variety of other mosses such as apple moss and wavy catharinea. I vividly remember my first trip into Mountain Maple Hollow with Roger Landers. It was after the fall color, mosses were vibrant, and there was that pungent smell of balsam and pine. In a sense, we had been transported to the forests of northeast Minnesota.

Perhaps we find Iowa's rocky outcrops all the more appealing because there are so few of them. The exploration of rocky environments is always an adventure. One learns what to expect on a given slope and exposure, but there are always exceptions and new discoveries. Rock as a substrate appears to be unyielding, yet a host of native plants colonize its surface, breaking it down into soil components.

Paradoxically, poor land management—which creates the conditions for exposure of new outcrops—needs to be avoided at all costs. In 1990 a soil scientist told me that topsoil was becoming increasingly difficult to find on slopes of the four northeast Iowa counties. As soil depth is reduced over shallow underlying bedrock, options for agricultural use diminish. Geologic erosion cannot be stopped, but we must take all necessary steps not to accelerate it by leaving fragile topsoils unprotected.

Tall blazing-stars, gray-headed coneflowers, and compass-plants along a prairie swale in virgin prairie at Doolittle Pothole Prairie, Story County.

Prairie Relicts

Tucked away in odd corners of the farm country's patchwork quilt, remnants of tallgrass prairie continue to flourish in unbroken sod. They are the last page of a grassland history, surviving only as tiny hemmed-in plots now tattered by alien plants and intrusions by landowners. Since re-creating a "native" prairie with its diverse plant community is still largely a pipe dream, what remains is virtually all we have. Prairie preservation has always been a monumental problem. The challenge continues today.

Before 1800, tallgrass prairie stretched from Ohio forest west to east central Nebraska and from Saskatchewan south to north Texas. It was a smooth, gently rolling grassland with endless vistas broken only by occasional cottonwood stands along streams, forested river valleys, and bur oak parklands. Prairie grasslands were open to the sun and the sky, which caused uneasiness in the early pioneers who had grown up in eastern woodlands. It was also a land of extremes: there was searing heat in summer, bitter cold during long winters, and shortages of water, fuel, and neighbors. When raging prairie fires were added to these hostilities, it is easy to see why Euro-American settlement proceeded at a snail's pace.

After early settlers learned the true wealth of the prairie soil, they made up for lost time.

In his research on the demise of Iowa prairie, University of Northern Iowa botanist Daryl Smith found that nearly all of Iowa's virgin prairie disappeared in the 70 years between 1830 and 1900 when Iowa was settled. Much of north central Iowa known geologically as the Wisconsin Lobe escaped intensive agriculture until the late 1880s when drainage ditches were dug and tile lines drained thousands of prairie pothole marshes and wet swales, converting them to prime agricultural land. Settlement proceeded from southeast Iowa along the major river courses and their tributaries toward the northwest. Much the same effect occurred from the Missouri River side of the state, where settlement proceeded toward the northeast. Very few roadless prairie tracts remained after 1910, save a small number in northwest Iowa. Most of Iowa's 29 million acres had either been plowed or would eventually be degraded by grazing. Iowa's tallgrass prairie covered about 83 percent of the state's total land area; today less than 2 percent remains.

Throughout the Midwest, islands of trees sprang up around farmsteads to mark prairie settlement. As the endless horizons vanished, so did the open feeling of true prairie. Where waving grasses once raced cloud shadows, endless rows of corn and soybeans now green the land. It is a landscape largely managed by farmers, but fragments of the old prairiescape still persist.

Relicts of tallgrass prairie vary in size from a fraction of an acre to quarter-section tracts. Often their identity as anything more than a shaggy "weed patch" is unknown to the landowner, although the use of prairie for hay still protects some of the larger areas. Individual and family interest has preserved some excellent areas, but small size, poor soil, very steep slopes, and poor drainage are the main reasons prairie fragments have remained intact.

Often the fate of protection for native land is a matter of current economics, politics, and individual priorities. When farmland

Pasqueflowers in dried grasses at Stinson Prairie State Preserve, Kossuth County.

is sold, new owners often have new ideas. "Swampbuster" legislation enacted in the 1980s has helped stop the draining of remaining prairie wetlands, but resistance has developed by some members of the farm community who see it as an infringement of private property rights.

Paradoxically, protecting our prairie heritage and maintaining the genetic diversity of native plants are not often farm priorities, although the potential exists for new crops in agriculture's future. Eastern gamagrass, a relative of corn that grows in southern Iowa prairies, may provide farmers with a perennial grain which is up to 30 percent protein. It has a seven- to eight-ton-per-acre yield of 11–15 percent protein forage and grows at an astonishing rate of up to two inches per day. The cup-plant, which is found throughout Iowa in wet prairies, has been used as a high-quality forage for cattle. Most of the research on this plant has been done in Europe and Russia.

Another prairie plant with high commercial value is the tall blazing-star. During the past 10 or so years, its magenta spike has become a commercial success for the cut-flower industry. Gardeners have also begun to plant it in perennial beds with species like black-eyed Susans, shasta daisies, and asters.

Because prairie plant communities have inherent stability due to thousands of years of adaptation, the Iowa Department of Transportation and many county engineers have recognized the value of roadside prairie plantings. They provide an attractive vigorous plant community that requires less maintenance than introduced grasses or legumes like crown-vetch and bird's-foot trefoil. Prairie plants will also establish in very poor soil, such as the glacial till found on many road grades.

Small triangular fields frequently occur where a railroad right-of-way runs obliquely through a section of land. These one- to three-acre plots have often remained in native vegetation because although pie slices are desirable on the dinner table, they are incon-

Downy phlox and white sage on an abandoned railroad right-of-way at Prairie Creek Wildlife Refuge, Marshall County.

venient as field boundaries when large modern equipment is used. These small prairies are rarely utilized for grazing because of their limited potential and continuous crop farming on all sides. If a creek or river should cross the land section and intersect the rail line, the possibility increases that prairie triangles may exist. I have walked through one such area in eastern Story County many times. Though small, it contains a great variety of species growing on its wet and dry sites.

The greatest scheme to preserve large, important segments of native prairie was accomplished inadvertently when railroads established right-of-ways across the land in the 1800s. In a study of the Swaledale Railroad Prairie in north central Iowa, Thomas Eddy located 247 plant species, most of which were prairie species, on a 1.5-mile section of railroad right-of-way. This study site, which included an adjacent 10-acre sand prairie, illustrates the potential richness of old rail lines. Railroad right-of-ways not only protect an excellent cross section of prairie flora but also often provide the only source of wildlife habitat in areas where cultivated crops abound. Some of this prairie may be in prime condition since former railroad maintenance consisted of annual burning, which increases the vigor and diversity of prairie flora and slows invading woody vegetation. Today the use of abandoned lines for hiking, biking, and horseback riding has protected some excellent prairie.

One abandoned rail line of the Chicago NorthWestern Railroad cut through the northeast corner of our farm. It was known as the Story City Branch and joined communities from Marshalltown west to Story City. As a youth, I considered it to be one of the truly wild areas on our central Iowa farm. To this day, it still stirs my curiosity.

One June morning in the early 1970s my father and I were hunting prairie flowers along the old railbed. Our walk took us through the delicate pinks and whites of downy phlox when I noticed a lavender-colored prairie spiderwort coming up between

Culver's root and cream gentian on the edge of a bur oak savanna along the Skunk River, Story County.

the ties outside the rails. We stumbled down a small embankment to the track bed, and I knelt down to study the spiderworts, which are half-day flowers that open shortly after sunrise and close in midday. My father poked on down the line to see what he could find. I had no more than settled down when he announced he had found a wild strawberry. I'm fond of flowers, especially the light magenta faces of prairie spiderworts, but the taste of a wild strawberry is hard to beat. With a sweet taste on my mind, I abandoned the spiderworts and hurried down the track to join him. We searched the area thoroughly but collected only a few berries. It was only the first week in June.

By the second week in June, the wild strawberries were prime. On two forays we had a hatful (a hatful, by the way, is about two quarts). The biggest berries were on those vines growing in the rock and cinders between the ties just outside the rails. There were others well out in the right-of-way, but the competition from the grass kept their berry-producing capacity at a minimum. For three weeks, we collected the abundance, ate strawberries and cream, and made jam and strawberry pies. Ten years later we purchased the right-of way from the railroad after its abandonment. Wild strawberries and prairie spiderworts still greet us in early June.

On the edge of Iowa's prairies, bur oak groves or parklands often extended into prairie grasslands and formed a community known as oak savanna. Bur oak has the unique ability to invade grasslands because the bark of mature trees is especially fire resistant and seedlings quickly resprout following fire. It is still possible to see these old trees on the south and west sides of native woods as one drives across Iowa. The nearly horizontal bottom branches on these open-grown oaks create spacious, spreading canopies as wide as the tree is tall. Savanna was not, however, just an open prairie landscape with large oaks. It contained a mixture of shrubs such as American wild plum, hazelbrush, and wild prairie crabapple. Cream gentian, Solomon's seal, carrion flower, and tinker's weed were characteristic forbs. There were also distinctive grasses such as Virginia wildrye and bottlebrush grass.

The generally open character of savanna was maintained by grazing and frequent fires. Since pioneer settlement, more than a century of fire suppression has enabled younger trees to grow up, around, and through the lower branches of these prairie giants. The shading effects of these saplings occasionally kills an open-grown tree or at least kills its lower, spreading branches, altering its original shape. Young oak-hickory forest has replaced prairie savanna throughout much of southern and eastern Iowa. Unlike native forest, it often lacks a diverse herbaceous understory. Ironically, many bur oak monarchs still exist where grazing has suppressed new forest growth.

A classic prairie savanna, Rochester Cemetery in Cedar County is one of the best examples of prairie and a cemetery coexisting. In the last week of May, prairie shooting-stars, wild columbine, downy phlox, mayapples, hoary puccoon, and Solomon's seals carpet the meadows between enormous open-grown bur oaks which may be more than 200 years old.

Abandoned cemeteries scattered across the land preserve pioneer history as well as prairie natural history. The dozen stones of one such graveyard near my home seem to reveal the true character of the pioneer era when they are surrounded by rainbow colors of summer flowers on a quiet day. Proper management of these tiny plots is of utmost importance since summer mowing reduces the vigor of native plants and encourages the invasion of perennial weeds.

Prairie relicts not only preserve native flora and provide prime wildlife habitat, they are also of great value to agriculture. Native prairie represents an endpoint in the development of priceless soils. Most of a prairie plant community is underground in massive root systems which gather water and nutrients. Roots of many species extend downward 10 feet or more, which protects the plants from seasonal variations in rainfall and from extremes such

Fruits of the American wild plum along a roadside near the Mississippi River, Jackson County.

as drought. The development of prairie soils favors humus accumulation, which occurs when the crowns and especially the roots of plants decay. Organic humus contains and holds water and nutrients. It is the chief reason for Iowa's agricultural productivity. Through continuous tilling of the soil, humus is oxidized and soil loses productivity. Thus virgin prairie soil is an index of original quality—an invaluable benchmark from which the effects of modern land use can be measured. Since native land is largely free from chemical additives, the influence of pesticides, herbicides, and chemical fertilizers can be examined and the activity of microorganisms, effects of soil compaction, and erosion rates can be compared. The worldwide importance of American farm products makes preservation of small prairie tracts for such studies imperative to agriculture's future.

Vast virgin prairie landscapes of Iowa are gone forever, but prairie patches live on, thriving in the nooks and crannies of a land plotted and planted. Thus the search for relict prairies provides all the excitement of a treasure hunt.

The history of no patch of prairie stands out in my mind more than a tiny gravel slope Roger Landers and I stumbled upon in northwest Iowa. Three prairie species—butterfly milkweed, Indian plantain, and the wood lily—vividly expressed the color of a prairie July, but there was only one plant of each. Along the little prairie's roadside border "No Spraying" signs stood guard. Another watcher had preceded us—the tiny scrap of prairie provided a connecting link which joined us together.

Compass-plants against cumulus clouds in the evening sky at Prairie Creek Wildlife Refuge, Marshall County.

Great Weather

No natural phenomenon affects people who work on the land as directly as weather. It determines what they do, where they go, and how they approach their jobs. As a naturalist, I have always been fascinated with the daily weather. It determines the future of the natural world and, because of its randomness, guarantees that no two years will be quite the same. We often hear that seasonal rainfall or daily temperatures are above or below normal, yet "normal" weather is really the sum total of a great variety of extremes.

My introduction to dramatic weather began at an early age. When I was seven years old I vividly remember a summer hail storm that wiped out our corn crop. My mother, my sister, and I were in the basement looking up the stairs at my father, who was standing with the backdoor open watching the action. He knew hail could shred his corn crop, but I believe he was also fascinated by the event. As soon as the storm had passed, he was preparing to deal with the outcome. There was not a lot of grumbling; hail had fallen, and nothing could be done about it. It was his attitude and curiosity which helped shape my own intrigue with weather.

In nature everything is based on the weather of the present

or of the past. Plants are affected directly and indirectly by rainfall, temperature, wind, and sunlight. We know that rain is essential, but today's society leads us to believe it should not be an inconvenience. Ideally, rain should come at night on a weekday, and sun should prevail from dawn till dusk, especially on weekends. We want control of the world about us. Weather is tolerated begrudgingly and is not always viewed with humble curiosity.

My greatest irritation with weather comes about not from the weather itself but from watching or listening to news forecasts and hearing a meteorologist tell me what kind of day we will experience and how we should feel about it. Rainy days are the epitome of gloom, and sunny weather is just perfect, that is, if it is not too hot or too cold. Some of this personal conjecture on the part of weather reporters may be just human nature, but their subtle suggestions lead many people away from an appreciation of weather's great diversity. The mixture of weather systems and the changes they bring gives us unique opportunities to see the world in new ways.

Dry weather is often as important as wet in maintaining the life cycles of plants and animals. In central Iowa, we experienced a severe drought in the summer of 1977. Groundwater reserves were low because of little rain in the fall of 1976 and no snow and sparse spring rains in 1977, yet some wild plants responded that summer with bountiful crops of fruit. Never before or since have I seen bigger or better-tasting wild plums. They were sweet, juicy, and insect free. It began to rain in early August, but the fruits had formed during the summer heat and drought. My father, who farmed for nearly 50 years, often said that years which were drier than average produced better corn crops.

Botanist John Pleasants believes that compass-plants respond with a large seed production the year following drought. Tree-ring research of past weather patterns indicates rainfall is above average the second year after a drought—the year in which the seeds would germinate and become established. Thus the compass-plant is sowing its progeny when there is better weather ahead.

Sky conditions tell us much about upcoming weather. The presence or absence of clouds indicates relative humidity, barometric pressure, and wind conditions. Cirrus are high-altitude clouds, generally above 16,500 feet, which consist of thin layers of ice crystals. They are composed of long, parallel streamers and blue sky is usually visible through the veil of white. Cirrus assume many shapes and forms; however, the best-known variety is called mares' tails because the ends of strands are hooked. They precede most low-pressure systems by 12 to 24 hours and are an indicator of change.

To the photographer, cirrus clouds present an opportunity to capture colorful sunrises or sunsets. Fifteen to 20 minutes before sunrise and 15 to 20 minutes after sunset, light rays pass through the layers of cirrus and produce a series of colors. At sunrise, it begins with the deepest magenta. Gradually it changes to red, then orange, yellow, and finally the white of cirrus. At sunset this color sequence occurs in reverse order. It is a very predictable event; however, since we cannot know what lies below the horizon or how heavy the cirrus layer is, the results can vary from breathtaking color to a solid gray that finally dims. Silhouettes of trees, flying geese, compass-plants, tall grasses, or other natural objects against a colorful cirrus sunset make dramatic photographs.

The clash between moisture-laden warm air and cold dry air can produce strong winds, heavy precipitation, hail, and possible tornadoes. Wall clouds can also result from this interaction. As a storm approached one summer morning, I anticipated some wild activity and drove to an open field just north of our farmstead to watch. Due west and northwest, a short gray-black cloud covered much of the horizon at the head of the storm. It appeared to be moving toward me without delay. I assumed it was a wall cloud and began to take photos. Increasing wind velocity made it difficult to stand, let alone keep the camera upright on its tripod. In a gust my hat was lifted from my head and disappeared over the truck

Wall cloud coming in from the west at Prairie Creek Wildlife Refuge, Marshall County.

into the distance. When the cloud appeared to be about one-half mile distant, I scrambled into my truck and headed for shelter, expecting higher winds and falling trees. Although little wind damage actually resulted, weather reports later confirmed a wall cloud had indeed passed through central Iowa. The experience was worth far more than the risk involved. (Later I was able to retrieve my somewhat muddy hat 50 yards downwind.)

When one lives in open country where the skyline is not blocked by tall trees, hills, or buildings, distant cumulonimbus clouds—more commonly called thunderheads—visibly mark the horizon many summer evenings. Anvils project from their tops when a cumulonimbus stops growing higher because of warm or dry, stable air above it. These towering clouds can grow to 60,000 feet, making them visible a hundred or more miles distant. When sidelit, their colossal forms are awe-inspiring.

Mammatus, or pocket, clouds sometimes form on the underside of an anvil. They indicate very moist upper atmospheric conditions with instability in the downward direction. Although mammatus signal the potential for violent weather, their appearance sunlit early or late in the day is that of puffy cotton balls.

In August 1977 a severe storm left our central Iowa farm under a dome of mammatus clouds. We could see the anvil form of this enormous cumulonimbus cloud only in the far south, although it was also directly above us and extended north to the horizon. Just before sunset a clearing had developed in the west. As the sun sank, the entire sky turned shades of yellow, pink, and red. In the years that have passed I have not seen a sunset sky which equals that single evening.

When a towering thunderhead passes overhead during the day, the light level drops as the cloud approaches and rain begins to fall. Early in July 1992 a thunderhead loomed large over our farm. About 11 A.M. the storm approached and the sky grew steadily darker until it appeared as dark as night when one looked out the

Trailing edge of a thunderstorm with mammatus clouds at sunset over
Prairie Creek Wildlife Refuge, Marshall County.

window. Was it as dark as my eyes seemed to tell me? I decided to measure the ambient, or available, light with a sensitive photographic light meter so I could compare it to the light level on an average cloudy day during a rainstorm. My meter has a scale which reads from one to 22. A reading of one is near the absence of perceivable light, and bright sunlight reads 20 on the scale. Each additional number means the light level is twice that of the preceding value. As you go from five to six, the light level doubles. From five to seven a four-fold increase occurs, and from five to eight, an eight-fold increase. Measurements of light levels I have taken in past rainstorms had read from nine to 14 on the scale. Overcast usually gives a reading of 14 to 16 and early morning shade, a reading of 12 to 15.

During what appeared to be the darkest period, I took a reading outside of our south door. The needle hovered at three. (Moonlight reflecting off snow also reads three on the scale.) It was by far the darkest period I have ever recorded during midday. The light level was 2,000 times lower than the light level beneath most heavy rainstorms when my meter reads 14, and 131,000 times lower than that of sunlight when the meter reads 20. Later that day, weather reports indicated that a solid cloud mass had extended from near the earth's surface to 60,000 feet, a distance of more than 11 miles.

As a photographer I often seek out calm weather conditions. Wind is the bane of long exposures, which are required when shooting in low light. Light wind or calm conditions may occur when the center of a high or low pressure system passes over. Wind also often lulls in the evening and throughout the night until vertical air currents develop in midmorning due to heating of the earth's surface. Thus I frequently find myself out at dawn and dusk.

Light pollution inhibits observation of the nighttime sky, the stars, and advancing storms for a majority of city people. Most rural areas in Iowa are still relatively free of this problem. I often walk at night to look at the sky, listen for animal sounds, and check weather conditions. One evening many large thunderheads loomed under the brilliant light of a full moon. They appeared ghost-like against the dark sky, with flashes of lightning illuminating their interiors.

Many years ago I was visiting at a friend's farm when we detected the thunder of an approaching storm. We hurried to an open field to watch its approach. Because the storm was moving slowly, we were able to observe constant streaks of lightning pass between the ground and the low clouds only a few miles away. It was one of my best opportunities to observe lightning and record it photographically.

Photographic possibilities are commonly dictated by weather conditions. When we have an early spring warm-up, trees, shrubs, and flowers may bloom weeks before their normal time. Fruiting trees caught by a late spring freeze may fail to produce fruit after such an event.

Autumn color is a product of photoperiod and weather. As the day length shortens, chlorophyll breaks down and sugars begin to build up in storage areas of leaf cells called vacuoles. This buildup of sugars favors the formation of anthocyanins and beta-cyanins, two water-soluble pigments. Depending on conditions within the leaf, cell sap may be acidic, which causes anthocyanins to appear red, or it may be basic, in which case they appear blue. Betacyanins are red pigments such as we see in tomatoes. When these underlying pigments are exposed by the loss of green chlorophyll, we see brilliant yellows, reds, and oranges.

Exceptional leaf color often occurs when there is a long series of clear warm days and cold, but not freezing, nights. Warm temperatures promote sugar formation within the leaf. This sugar is then transported to the trunk and roots of the plant for storage; however, when nights cool quickly, the transport of sugars is slowed and more sugar is left in the leaves, where it is converted to anthocyanins.

In 1991 freezing temperatures killed the green leaves on

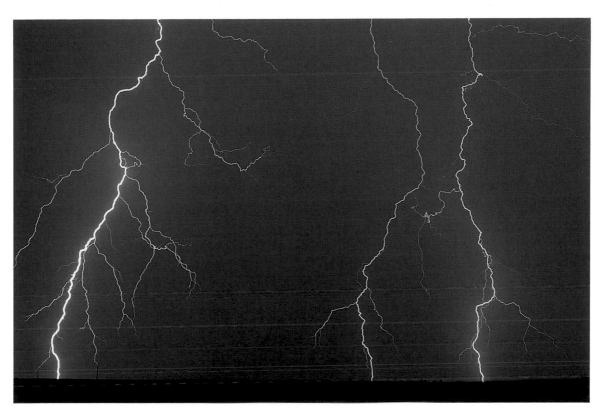

Lightning bolts at the leading edge of an approaching storm about 10:00 P.M. in eastern Story County.

many trees over much of Iowa and Minnesota. As a result there was little color; the leaves simply dried up and fell off. Only where temperatures were moderated by land features or bodies of water did brilliant autumn colors occur. The 1991 freeze also affected trees in 1992 since it injured cambium tissue, which makes sapwood for the next season. During the 1992 season, stressed trees struggled with less than the normal amount of this water-conducting tissue. The response to this event was summer defoliation and browning of leaves in some species; others began to change color several weeks to a month ahead of their normal schedules.

Precise temperature and moisture conditions create a coating of frost which magically transforms ordinary winter landscapes into crystalline wonderlands. Each frost may appear similar to the casual observer, but two basic types exist.

Rime frost, sometimes called rime ice, occurs when supercooled fog droplets (still liquid, but below 32° F) freeze onto exposed objects. Rime frost often accompanies winter fog to cover grass, trees, and bushes.

Hoarfrost, a frozen version of dew, forms by sublimation (a process where ice turns directly into water vapor or water vapor turns directly into ice without going through a liquid state). Hoarfrost commonly forms on the surface of ice, grass, leaves, or soil on very cold, clear nights when there is a high loss of radiant heat. It can also form where there is very moist air, such as entrances to active animal burrows.

Spicular and tabular are two common types of crystal structures. Spicular crystals are needle-like and often occur in late autumn and early spring. Tabular crystals are broad, flat, and pointed, like feathers. I have found large circular clusters of tabular hoarfrost on clear lake ice when the temperature had fallen below −10° F. Early one morning on open ice just above a beaver dam, I observed an amazing array of crystal "feathers," each nearly 1.5 inches in length.

Tabular hoarfrost at sunset on the open ice of Middle Minerva Creek, Marshall County.

Hoarfrost and rime frost are spawned by cold, damp climatic conditions when the weather is otherwise stable, while ice storms are caused by unstable weather. Winter snowstorms and ice storms are usually caused by opposite conditions and do not occur concurrently. A cold front coming down from the north brings a snowstorm, while a warm front moving up from the south produces the conditions for an ice storm.

When I awoke one winter morning it was spitting rain. The temperature hovered at the freezing mark, and ice had already begun to form on the trees, fences, and powerlines. The forecasters had warned us it was coming. Rain, ice, sleet, and snow had all been in their predictions. There wasn't a single bird feeding in the front yard while I ate breakfast. When I stuck my head out the backdoor, cold rain, driven by a bitter north wind, smacked me in the face. It left little to the imagination.

Weather maps the night before had shown a warm front creeping up from the southwest. It was due to meet, right in our area, with a cold front edging down from the north. Thus the conditions were ripe for an ice storm. The moist air on the leading edge of the cold front would rise, condense, fall as rain, and then freeze as it struck objects on the ground.

In less than an hour every branch, twig, bud, and wire was encapsulated in a clear case of ice. The deciduous silver and sugar maple trees bore up under the weight rather well, but the redcedars and old Norway spruces along our lane began drooping badly and soon their crowns were nodding.

By midmorning a rain-soaked window pane on the north side of our house was covered with bits of ice. Since sleet freezes before it strikes the earth, the upper air temperature was apparently dropping slightly. This was a good sign. If the freezing rain continued, the buildup of ice could cause severe tree damage, to say nothing of downed utility lines and the inconvenience caused by a power blackout.

When it appeared the rain had changed entirely to sleet, I ventured out to look around. The grass and fallen leaves were frozen stiff and crunched underfoot. The air was filled with tiny ice pellets that hammered against my face with stinging blows. Looking skyward was out of the question. The sidewalk was as slick as glass, and the sleet ricocheted bullet-like from its surface. The sleet had no more than completely replaced the rain when flakes of snow began to appear.

By lunchtime the ground was all white. Walking near the north edge of our grove, I stopped behind a shed to watch the driving snow. The old silver maples in our grove stood stark and seemingly lifeless. The north sides of their trunks were plastered with ice and snow, but they remained wet and black as coal on the leeward side. The wind gusted throughout the afternoon, frequently whipping the snow into a blinding blizzard. Occasionally an overweight tree branch would break with a rifle-like crack and drop. The crash sent ice flying like broken glass in all directions. By 8:00 P.M., the snow had reduced to flurries but continued throughout the night and much of the next day.

Two days after the storm I watched the sun rise bright and clear above a disappearing cloud bank on the eastern horizon. It was a welcome sight after the cloudy days, even though the relentless wind continued. Birds also rejoiced in the sun's reappearance. Our feeders had standing room only and were covered with jays and juncos, a pair of cardinals, and three different species of woodpeckers.

In mid-January on a bitter cold, windy, gray day the return of spring hardly seems possible. Yet it is the duration of winter's weather, its difficulties, and the hardships it imposes that brings us the hope and promise of spring.

Our first snowfall often comes in early November, signaling the official start of the winter season. The sun's rays are already striking the earth at an oblique angle. Their power to warm the land has not only diminished, but the day's length has also shortened as the sun moves toward the winter solstice. Temperatures ease downward until daytime highs fail to reach the freezing point. Lakes and marshes freeze first, then the streams, and finally the rivers. New ice is thin and transparent, but as the cold deepens, ice thickens and becomes chalky white and firm enough to support an automobile. Only the occasional riffle from a feeder stream, a rapids, or an underwater spring keeps water from freezing. The land and its watery environs appear to be nearly barren of life. An aura of silence prevails; even human activities diminish. Winter may exert its icy grip for more than five months.

The signs of spring are subtle at first, scarcely noticed by all but the most observant. During the relative warmth of midday, the cardinal's whistle heralds that change is imminent. He may sing on rare occasions in December, but usually it is after a winter warm spell (often called the January thaw, even if it occurs in February) that his song becomes a regular midday feature. The cardinal's nesting season is still nearly five months away, but his territorial imperative seems to say "plan ahead." By early February, the great horned owl has built its nest and begun to lay a clutch of eggs. With snowstorms likely and below-freezing temperatures virtually guaranteed, incubation must be nearly free from interruption. In early March, the eggs have hatched and the young birds beg for food, requiring almost constant protection from a brooding parent. By mid-March, the pointed hoods of skunk cabbage emerge in a woodland bog, melting the snow with their internal heat.

For most of us, the spring does not begin with the great horned owl's nesting, the cardinal's first song, or the appearance of skunk cabbage. It is when we feel the heat of the spring sun on our backs and we see a patch of green in a snow-covered lawn. Yet the sure sign that the spring thaw has arrived occurs when the lakes, marshes, rivers, and streams are free of ice.

The melting of lake and river ice can occur as early as February, or as late as mid-April near the Minnesota border. Many variables, such as air temperature, solar radiation, water temperature from inflowing streams, water depth, and rate of flow, are contributing factors. Whether the breakup is early or late simply depends on how much heat is available. In the case of ice, "latent heat" is needed. It is the amount of heat required to convert ice back to the liquid state without changing its temperature. It is considerably less than the amount of heat required to turn boiling water into steam, but it is about the same amount of heat as is needed to bring lukewarm water to the boiling point.

As ice melts, it changes from chalky white to a greenish gray and has a thin sheet of water forming over its surface. Although this color change and gradual melting may occur over a period of days or even weeks, ice can be with us one day and gone the next. This has led to the mistaken notion that ice can somehow become heavier than water and sink.

Of course, we know that ice floats, but to understand how it can melt so quickly, we must first look at the freezing process. Freezing water molecules form an open latticework of crystals, so the solid is less dense and lighter than the liquid. As crystals form, they also exclude some impurities such as silt, minerals, or pollutants. These accumulate along the sides of each crystal and may be called brine pockets. However, after ice thickens, an incubation period may cause the crystal structure to change. Studies have shown that crystals may grow by themselves or that small crystals may fuse to form larger ones.

Long, columnar crystals are known to form beneath the surface of river and lake ice. They may attain a size of 2.5 centimeters (one inch) in diameter and up to 30 centimeters (about one foot) in length. Because they align themselves vertically with the brine pockets forming the planes of weakness between them, they have been given the common name of "candle ice."

When melting occurs, the brine pockets enlarge and eventually make contact with the surface meltwater. Then the transport of heat by convection can occur throughout the ice cover. A critical point is reached when liquid water surrounds each "candle" and the entire ice sheet, or perhaps loose floating blocks of the ice that have been broken up by the mechanical action of wind or currents, disintegrates into a mush of crystalline ice. At this point, water movement promotes a rapid exchange of latent heat and ice crystals melt quickly. The remains of the ice sheet can be reduced in a matter of hours to a few crystals that lap against the rocks of a lakeshore or brush along a river bank, drifting with the current. I have watched ice break up in a small pond when a stiff wind blows. Stronger wave action aids the breakup. As the ice mass disintegrates into small chunks of vertical crystals, they chink and rattle as they form a slush on the trailing edge of the intact ice sheet.

It is a revelation when the ice goes. We can feel it in our bones, knowing that as the days lengthen migrating birds will arrive to serenade the dawn. First there are Canada geese in long wavy lines, then ducks feeding in the fields, and red-winged blackbirds on territorial perches. In the woods hepatica poke through the leaf layer over newly thawed earth, and the pale blue of pasqueflowers promises resurrection on a windy glacial esker. In a matter of weeks, reddish willow twigs turn green along rivers and streams. At first there are just a few events occurring each day and we can hardly wait to take them in. But as spring advances, new birds arrive and flowers bloom with increasing frequency. Spring is a season without hesitation when it fully comes about, and winter becomes a distant memory.

Pectoral sandpiper in the north pond at Prairie Creek Wildlife Refuge, Marshall County.

The Bird Habit

Those of us who watch birds often do so unconsciously as we go about our daily lives. Whether we are traveling or eating at the kitchen table, we observe their activities. Birds tell us a great deal about the world around us. Their feeding behavior may indicate pending weather conditions, the presence or absence of certain species denotes the season of the year, and bird songs can tell us the time of day. Nature appreciation for many people begins by watching birds. For some, birding is a casual pastime; others deem it a constant challenge, a lifelong numbers game with a "life list." Serious birders plan vacations to see new species in exotic locations. Their records on each species, its location, and the number of individuals contribute important information to the scientific community.

Roger Tory Peterson calls birds an "environmental litmus paper." Where birds are doing well, the environment is healthy not only for birds but also for human inhabitants. When environmental conditions deteriorate, birds may still be present but the striking variety of bird species characteristic of a healthy environment no longer exists.

It might be easy to conclude that birds couldn't care less about people, yet these avian animals do respond to human activity by coming to feeders and nest boxes. Their songs lift our hearts and minds and renew our spirits. Many individuals nurture and protect the world at large simply because there are birds that depend on natural environments.

As a youngster in rural Iowa I was most aware of farm-related birds. Pigeons or rock doves lived in our barn loft, house sparrows and European starlings sought spilled grain in our livestock lots, pheasants flushed as we harvested corn in the fall, and mallards flew along our creek to an old oxbow lake north of our farm, where I hunted them at dusk. One exception to these common birds was a kestrel which roosted during the winter months beneath the eaves on the north side of our barn. When I was doing evening chores, he would dive from his perch and alight in a nearby walnut tree. He always remained alert and distant until I departed. Western meadowlarks occasionally came to the cowyard in winter. Through the spring and summer, the clear notes of their songs echoed across our pasture from distant fence posts.

Behind our house a small orchard contained a number of red cherry trees. Since we relished cherry pies, I was somewhat defensive of the ripening fruit, warding off red-headed woodpeckers that seemed to glean the ripest cherries from the tops of the trees. It proved to be a losing proposition, as the birds were persistent and returned immediately after I left the orchard. Finally my father observed that the birds' cherry picking stopped when the mulberries ripened. From that point on, we took the matter less seriously. Years later I photographed red-heads during mulberry season; their pristine white fronts were stained purple and they had juice and seeds around their beaks.

I saw bluebirds and goldfinches in an old lilac near our house, but this was unusual and I assumed that few of these birds existed. My parents were not serious birders, but my father was a keen observer. He may not have known correct bird names, but he recognized different species. One fall during the harvest season he found an injured red-tailed hawk along our creek. It had a bullet wound through its wing and was unable to fly. We covered the front of an old crate with wire mesh to make a cage and fed it until it could fly.

When my eyes were first opened to the world of birds, I asked, "How did I previously fail to notice these colorful feathered critters? Were they always present?" It was not until I was in college majoring in fisheries and wildlife biology that I saw my first slate-colored junco, now called the dark-eyed junco. I had scattered some grain outside our picture window to attract birds. They scratched for seeds as the season's first snow settled gently. These were "snowbirds." In my senior year I spent a warm spring morning in Ames along Squaw Creek in Brookside Park watching an American redstart. He spent most of his time flying from a sunlit logjam in midstream to catch insects. It was my first warbler sighting; I remember it well, since I should have been studying for finals.

After military service in the late 1960s, I began to watch birds earnestly. Most mornings I walked around our farm grove to keep abreast of their changing activity. In a few years I knew which species to expect during each season; thus birding was an opportunity to renew old acquaintances and make new friends.

Through the years we have planted grasses, flowers, trees, and shrubs to create wildlife habitat on our farm. The most dramatic change occurred when we planted two small crop fields adjacent to our farmstead and a 25-acre pasture to tall prairie grasses. The prairie seems to have affected the number and type of birds we now observe. The sedge wren did not inhabit our land, but now it is one of our most abundant grassland birds.

During the early and mid-1970s the bobolink was common in our smooth brome–bluegrass pasture; today it is rare. Had tall grasses and the absence of grazing discouraged bobolinks, or were other factors responsible? My neighbor's 60-acre grazed pasture also had many pairs; in the mid-1990s only one or two pairs remain.

Ornithological research seems to indicate a problem in Central and South America, where wintering and migrating bobolinks and dickcissels feed and roost in large flocks. Because they feed in grainfields, they are seen as pests and are eradicated whenever possible. I continue to hope for the bobolink's future and wonder if the type of grassland could make a difference.

Our first prairie plantings were dense stands of tall grasses, while recent reconstructions are mixtures of flowers and short and tall grasses. During the past several years I have seen occasional bobolinks in early spring, but so far they appear to be migrants. The male is the only North American land bird that is light above and dark below. Because of this coloration he has been called the "skunkbird." He is one of my favorites; his song tinkles like a wind chime as he wings over a prairie meadow. I have heard recently that the Conservation Reserve Program has dramatically bolstered bobolink numbers in some areas. I can only hope for their future.

Our old farm grove has always contained a number of resident birds. Great horned owls roosted and nested in snags of old silver maples which were planted about the turn of the century. During the mid-1980s, however, we began to hear the wild "Who cooks for you" call of barred owls at twilight, midnight, and midday. In early summer, a strange new call emanated from the leafy canopy. With serious searching, Linda found its source: young barred owls that continually announced their presence so their parents could locate them. The growing youngsters provided an unexpected bonus when they began to spend time directly behind our house. At 8:45 P.M. one June evening we observed two juveniles, six to eight weeks old, in low branches of a large black maple near our garden. They were chasing a cottontail rabbit around a lilac bush. Like most young predators, their skills needed considerable honing. When the rabbit finally went under a dense canopy of peonies, the owls split up; one watched from one side, one from the other. The rabbit's re-emergence brought both owls to the ground in pursuit.

Juvenile barred owl at Prairie Creek Wildlife Refuge, Marshall County.

The chase consisted of short flights, alighting, and hopping along on the ground. The rabbit again retreated to the cover of the peonies. As we watched, it appeared that the sibling owls had given up the chase. Even the rabbit seemed to sense the game was up, but when he came back out into the open, one owl immediately left his perch and nearly connected. The cottontail jumped three feet straight up, evading the owl, and headed for protection beneath the low boughs of a blue spruce. It was nearly dark; perhaps the game of owl and rabbit continued in darkness, but we were unable to watch. Other evenings we watched the pair of young owls bathe in our birdbath, a flat container lying on the ground. Owls batheing was not something we expected!

Great horned owls are known to prey on barred owls, but we have never observed or heard a great horned in our woodland since the barred owls took up residence. Why did one owl species apparently displace the other? Did the barred owls evict the great horned owls or did they leave because there was a change in available food supply due to increased presence of adjacent grassland? On numerous occasions we have observed barred owls foraging for deer mice and meadow voles. They prefer low branches where prairie meets the woodland. We suspect that habitat change altered the food supply and that the two species have dramatically different needs.

One winter evening well after dark I was taking kitchen scraps to our compost pile when the sound of a distressed cardinal came from a nearby stand of conifers. In our yard light I watched a flying cardinal just evade a pursuing barred owl. Recently we have seen a barred owl perched near the compost pile. Perhaps cardinal is on his menu. Another wrinkle in this owl mystery was the disappearance of screech owls about the same time the barred owls arrived. Occasionally we have again heard and seen screech owls. Are screech owls prey to both larger owl species?

Subtle bird behavior may be as interesting as dramatic action. One midwinter day I watched half a dozen tree sparrows and dark-eyed juncos sitting hunched and motionless on the leeward side of an old stand of redcedars. They reminded me of withered winter apples waiting for cedar waxwings. Their heads appeared as mere knobs with snowflakes settling softly on fluffed body feathers. There was little movement in the gang, although their heads occasionally turned like turrets scanning for danger. From half a dozen paces, I studied these tiny balls of life for what seemed to be an hour but was probably no more than five minutes. My presence began to cause uneasiness among the group. The closest bird stood up, stretched one leg, then the other, then both wings. Finally he turned 180 degrees on his slender perch and flew with the other members of his band.

One of the earliest signs of spring is seeing a robin in the backyard. These early robins confirm that winter is waning. Late one morning in mid-February we saw our first American robin, just outside my office window, sifting through piles of leaves. His spring breeding plumage was brilliant, with a pronounced white eye-ring. Ashy gray feathers covered his back, with rust in the upper wing coverts. White spots on the end of the outer feathers accented his charcoal-colored tail. His stiletto-tipped bill was orange and blackened at the point.

We marveled as he tugged, pulled, and tossed the dry leaves, looking for insects, larvae, grubs, or seeds. Many of the leaves were light and fluffy, but some were frozen down. These required considerable pulling to free them from their moorings and broke loose in large wads with snow, ice, and grass attached. The robin seemed to be quite successful in his quest for food and was soon joined by six or seven starlings. They apparently sensed he had a good thing going. The starlings' behavior was quite different from this early robin's. The robin sorted leaves to forage, often standing in an area he had cleared, tilting his head, perhaps listening as he looked at the ground, while the starlings poked their heads under leaves and rooted around like pigs, spreading their beaks as they searched.

American robin in early spring migration at Prairie Creek Wildlife Refuge, Marshall County.

Unlike the robin, they never picked up leaves and tossed them out of the way. The robin was apparently far more successful in his search, for the starlings soon moved to another part of the lawn and then abandoned the area altogether to eat beneath a bird feeder in the front yard.

Our robin was back several days later, but three or four inches of snow had fallen overnight and he was eating corn on our backyard bird feeder. We watched him for half an hour as he defended the feeder from sparrows, juncos, starlings, and cardinals. When the going got rough, mixed birdseed and corn would substitute for worms and insects anytime. Many years ago I also observed a dozen robins feeding on mixed birdseed behind our house after a spring ice storm.

Our curiosity teaches us much about bird behavior. Many questions arise as we watch birds, one of which is, Where do birds go at night? On occasion we see a bird going to roost, but it's a rare event. One evening in early May I was searching for warblers when I saw a rose-breasted grosbeak and a northern oriole fly into the leafy canopy of an American elm. They settled securely upon a branch and tucked their heads beneath their wings. I continued to watch them until darkness obscured my view, but they never moved. They had found a sleeping perch and would spend the night waving in the gentle breeze.

In the northern states, few birds would survive a winter night without proper protection, especially when the temperature falls below zero and is accompanied by a 30-mile-per-hour wind. Nuthatches and chickadees generally seek the protection of an old woodpecker cavity or birdhouse. One winter evening we watched a brown creeper in the virgin forest of Dows State Preserve. He approached an old red oak shortly after sundown and disappeared into a small, almost invisible hole some 15 or 20 feet above the ground. Jays, juncos, and cardinals usually seek the shelter of a protective spruce, pine, or cedar. Large hawks such as the red-tail and rough-leg also seek cover in coniferous windbreaks. Crows, on the other hand, may simply roost on branches in the open near the tops of deciduous trees, although in severe weather they too seek shelter in spruce or pine groves.

As I walked about one winter evening, there was a glowing fire in the sunset sky when I flushed a cock pheasant from his roost in the heart of an old redcedar. He had perched about 10 feet off the ground in the west central part of our grove. His departure came with such a clamor that both my dog Ruff and I were a bit startled. It was as if the tree itself had come to life. Boughs swayed as the boisterous fellow headed up through leafless silver maples and headed for parts unknown.

Winter feeding of birds always provides an opportunity to learn about new behavior. Bad weather often brings crows to our yard. One wet morning in late March three crows came to eat bird-seed and suet. It had been raining and their black plumage reflected the gray overcast. They wandered about on the ground picking up cracked corn rather than whole kernels. We watched them search for just the right piece. They were always alert, and after five minutes or so they suddenly headed off one by one into the wind and rain. When the weather is bad, hunger apparently takes precedence over the crow's typically wary nature.

Often our best observations of bird behavior occur when we least expect them. In late April 1993 we were returning from a controlled prairie burn just after 1:00 P.M. on a sunny, but cool, April afternoon. As we headed into our farm driveway I noticed a flurry of bird activity up about 10 feet on the trunk of an old black maple. We drove close to the tree and discovered that holes bored by a yellow-bellied sapsucker were oozing sap and the leeward side of the trunk was covered with large flies, sweat bees, and honeybees drinking the dilute maple syrup. In the branches of two small trees near the old monarch, ruby-crowned and golden-crowned kinglets were darting in and out, snatching flies from the trunk, making

Ruby-crowned kinglet at Prairie Creek Wildlife Refuge, Marshall County.

midair catches, or drinking sap. A stiff southeast wind confined their activity to the west side of the tree.

Kinglets are notorious for their flighty behavior; thus it dawned on me that this might be a long-awaited opportunity to photograph them. I immediately went to the house for a camera with a 400-mm telephoto lens, a long extension tube so the telephoto lens would be close-focusing, and an electronic flash. It took about an hour to go through the first 36-exposure roll. At about 2:30 P.M. I decided to break for lunch. The birds had grown used to my presence about 10 feet from the tree and were responding to the bait in increasing numbers. About an hour later I headed back to the tree, accompanied by my wife, Linda. She brought her sketch pad and sat down next to me in the ditch. At 4:00 P.M. the battery on the flash died, and I was down another roll of film. I went to the house to get additional film.

When I returned, the sun was lower in the west and photography was possible without the flash. Next to the old tree was a woven-wire fence where the birds frequently perched. They worked their way across, up, and down the wires and sometimes stopped momentarily. They also came out into the grass and leaves of the ditch to forage. As time passed, the activity would gradually wane until only a single ruby-crowned kinglet remained. Then, overhead, we would hear the high-pitched calls from another wave of golden-crowns. Soon they were darting in and out or clinging to the trunk as they foraged. Often there were territorial disputes. The ruby-crowned kinglets found this feeding site worth defending. They flashed their crowns to defend their perches from other ruby-crowns as well as the golden-crowns. They caught and ate the sweat bees whenever there was an opportunity, but there were few arguments with the honeybees and the birds could be seen veering away from them.

While we were watching the kinglets, a brown creeper came to the tree. I could hardly believe it, as creepers are very difficult to approach. Before the afternoon was over, two brown creepers were going up and (occasionally) down the tree stuffing themselves. They moved erratically and were very difficult to follow with the camera. At 6:30 P.M. the fifth 36-exposure roll of film had gone through the camera, we had gotten cold, the light was getting dim, and the cooling temperatures had reduced the number of flies on the trunk.

It had been an eventful afternoon, made possible by a number of circumstances. The late spring and the sapsucker holes had provided the sap for the insects. The sunlight and warm temperatures had increased insect activity, which was bait for the birds. A strong southeast wind seemed to confine the action to the west side of the tree, where it could be easily observed. It was quite likely a once-in-a-lifetime opportunity. We were seeing the interconnectedness of the food chain in action.

Spring is by far the most exciting time to observe birds as they come back from southern wintering areas. By early April, the Harris's, white-throated, and fox sparrows can be heard singing as they stop to feed during migration. They may come to feeders but are more likely to be seen in brushy woodlands, scratching through the duff and leaves.

One half of more than 30 warbler species that pass through Iowa settle within the state to raise their families. The remainder fly on to northern coniferous forests, gleaning newly hatched insects and larvae from trees as they go. Most warblers possess striking color combinations. The main colors are yellow, black, blue, and green, though splotches, streaks, or hoods of red, gray, orange, brown, or white decorate most species. Warblers often go through in waves. Their tiny flitting bodies appear is if by magic on bright mornings, filling the trees of town and country, backwoods and backyards. First arrivals of most species are seen among the new leaves of late April or early May.

As a young diehard birder, I sought warblers with enthusi-

Yellow-rumped warbler in a black maple during spring migration at Prairie Creek Wildlife Refuge, Marshall County.

asm. In 1971 it began on April 26 when I saw four or five pairs of yellow-rumped warblers while making my morning rounds of our farmstead. By the 29th, "Myrts" (yellow-rumped was formerly the Myrtle warbler) could be seen by the dozen in the trees everywhere. On May 5, I found the palm warbler—marked by his tiny rusty cap—feeding on the ground along a roadside. The 7th brought the yellowthroat, which nests throughout the state in moist sites with tall vegetation. On the 8th, orange-crowned and Nashville warblers were feeding on small green worms in our front yard maples. May 9 brought the chestnut-sided and the yellow warbler, which has red streaks up and down its breast. On the 11th, the trees were filled with Tennessee warblers, the black-and-white, the Cape May, the Blackburnian (with his orange throat), the blackpoll, the ovenbird, and the American redstart. All had arrived in the night. On the 12th, apple blossoms provided the background for a black-throated green and a magnolia warbler. Near dusk on the 14th, a yellow-breasted chat, the common yellowthroat's larger look-alike cousin, was along the north edge of our grove. On the 16th, while I was watching three scarlet tanagers in a small timber, a bay-breasted warbler appeared and just as promptly disappeared. On May 21, I was searching for nests in the same timber and came upon my first mourning warbler. Its appearance marked the season's end. The migrating warblers were gone. Through persistent searching, I had viewed 18 species of warblers in less than a month. To birders, warblers are the life and color of spring.

Most backyard species such as cardinals, thrashers, catbirds, and blue jays have adapted well to human intrusions. They live in our backyards, hedgerows, and farm windbreaks. However, many Neotropical migrants—that is, species which spend the winter in the Caribbean, Mexico, Central, or South America—appear to be declining in number. These include species such as northern and orchard orioles, eastern kingbirds, wood thrushes, scarlet tanagers, and warblers. While eastern kingbirds and northern and orchard orioles use edge habitats, many species require large, unbroken forest tracts. In such forests, ovenbirds nest on the forest floor, wood thrushes in the understory, and cerulean warblers in tree canopies. Birds of interior forests may not be able to compete with edge species such as house wrens and robins. The breakup of contiguous woodland is called "habitat fragmentation" and occurs with the building of trails, roads, and homesites. It may eliminate available nest sites due to structural changes within the woodland, encourage parasitism by the brown-headed cowbird, or increase the incidence of predation by house cats and raccoons. Only the protection of winter habitat in tropical areas as well as nesting habitat here in Iowa will assure a future for these species.

After we develop the "bird habit," an evening walk in early summer can take in the world around us. A growing chorus of bird song enhances the peaceful solitude. As the light fades robins and red-headed woodpeckers begin to scold in the woods. Across the road a yellowthroat sings "wichity wichity" from tall grasses in a wet ditch, while a song sparrow claims his right to an old fencerow along a neighbor's field. High overhead a bird warbles about territorial boundaries. It is but a tiny black speck high on the spire of an old Norway spruce. When he suddenly disappears, I feel no further need of pursuit, for binoculars or perfect light are not required to identify the repeating phrases of the indigo bunting. Like many other birds, his song and behavior, after more than 20 years of watching and listening, have become an indelible part of summer.

Yucca, leadplant, nineanther dalea, and big bluestem at Mount Talbot State Preserve, Woodbury County.

Iowa's West Coast

Bold bluffs stand out in abrupt relief against the adjacent
Missouri River floodplain in western Iowa. With flowing
contours accentuated by sharp-crested ridges and precipitous
slopes, they give the impression of a worn-down mountain range
stretching from central Plymouth County southward to the state line.

The Loess Hills, as the bluffs are known, form an impressive
corrugated topography about 160 miles in length, unbroken save
for those places where tributary valleys enter the broad Missouri
floodplain. From every high point, it is easy to understand why
these headland hills that conform irregularly to the course of the
river may be considered Iowa's west coast.

This hill range, created by windblown silt known as loess,
represents an unusual geological landform expressed here in one of
the two most dramatic examples in the world. (The other is in the
Kansu Province of northern China.) Loess, an important soil parent
material, forms about 40 percent of Iowa's best cropland. However,
only along the eastern edge of the Missouri floodplain does it lie in
60- to 200-foot-deep eroded drifts.

The steep bluffs were formed by loess deposition, a phenomenon which occurred for the most part over a period of nearly

20,000 years and ended about 12,500 years ago during the Pleistocene, the last known period of glaciation in Iowa. Essentially, meltwater from the glacial ice mass deposited sediments on the braided river floodplain. When melting slowed during cold weather, water receded from much of the floodplain, leaving it dry and barren.

Exposed to the strong prevailing winds from the west and northwest, the fine sediments were lifted into great dust clouds and carried downwind to the east. As these silt-laden winds encountered the slope of the river valley's east wall, their air currents broke formation and dropped their silty loads, much in the same manner as snowdrifts pile up behind snow fences. Small accumulations of loess were also deposited on the west side of the river when the winds shifted to a south or southwesterly direction; some of the thickest deposits west of the Missouri River are just north and south of the city of Omaha. Coarse, heavy silt accumulated near the floodplain, while finer silt and clay particles traveled farther. Measurable loess accumulated up to 160 miles downwind and was probably deposited during thousands of Pleistocene winters.

When the glacier retreated, there was no longer a source of sediment and loess deposition stopped. It seems reasonable that a protective covering of vegetation eventually grew over the floodplain; however, geologists point out that we do not know how soon this occurred or whether it was forest or grassland. In time, erosion started its wearing-down process and created the intricate, dune-like landscape we see today.

Loess is a powdery substance consisting primarily of silt particles of calcite or feldspar, small amounts of clay, and traces of fine sand. Highly erodible because of its fine texture and porous nature, undisturbed loess nonetheless exhibits a unique cohesiveness which allows it to stand easily in a vertical face such as a road cut. Natural vertical exposures are uncommon, although many bluff slopes will exceed a grade of 45 percent. On moderately steep slopes, there is often a series of horizontal shelves, called "cat steps," which have been formed by the natural slippage of water-soaked loess along the joint planes. They are often much more pronounced in areas where there is moderate to heavy grazing.

The first known scientific investigation of the Loess Hills region occurred in the early nineteenth century when Iowa was still a territory. The English naturalist Bradbury traveled in America from 1809 to 1811. In a later description of his ventures, he reported collecting plants on the eastern side of the Missouri (opposite the mouth of what is now Nebraska's Papillion River) and wading through what is known today as Folsom Lake to reach the unusual bluffs. About 1900, Louis Pammel, professor of botany at Iowa State University, prepared a list of plants from the region. Nine years later, Bohumil Shimek, head of the botany department at the University of Iowa, undertook a comprehensive survey of western Iowa vegetation.

When pioneers first came to the area, they settled in the valley bottoms along streams to be close to sources of water and wood. They obtained wood for building and burning as fuel from ravines and the forested north-facing slopes. The slopes facing east, south, and west were commonly prairie-covered. Although crops of corn and wheat were probably attempted on some slopes, crop failures due to summer heat and periodic dry weather likely encouraged many landowners to return these uplands to pasture or to cut the prairie grass for hay. Today, most of the steep slopes remain in native vegetation, while wide ridgetops and lowlands are generally under cultivation.

The native prairie which continues to thrive on many of the exposed slopes is one of the region's attractive features. Before pioneer settlement, grasses covered far more of the Loess Hills landscape. Seasonal fires which raged over much of the Great Plains helped to maintain the prairie's vigor and stay the advance of woodlands, but cultivation of the land stopped the cleansing effect of periodic fires. In their absence, many slopes have been invaded by redcedar and woody shrubs such as sumac and dogwood.

Forest succession eventually crowds out the shade-intolerant prairie plants. Still, the prairie persists, its survival aided greatly by the drying effect of hot southwesterly summer winds. On south-facing slopes, they create a near desert-like climate inhospitable to temperate forests.

One sunny July afternoon I performed a simple experiment. I took temperature readings on two opposing slopes—one was south-facing and prairie-covered, the other north-facing and forested. Two readings were taken in each area—one at ground level, the other three feet above the ground.

Between two tussocks of little bluestem on the south-facing prairie slope the mercury soared to 145° F, while the three-foot reading was 93° F. On the opposing north-facing slope, in a dry streambed 50 yards into a shady forest, both readings were 83° F. Thus, the ground-level readings differed by 62 degrees, the three-foot readings by only 10 degrees. Undoubtedly, temperature differences exercise some control over the balance of prairie and woodland.

Transition zones between forest and prairie frequently contain green ash, rough-leaf dogwood, and smooth sumac, which reddens hillsides in autumn. Bur oak is also common on the forest uplands and is often mixed with basswood and red oak.

As might be expected, the flora of the Loess Hills represents a great diversity of species. More drought-resistant than woody vegetation, prairie grasses such as little bluestem and side-oats grama dominate the upper slopes. Big bluestem, Indian grass, and switchgrass prevail at the moist lower levels.

Numerous prairie flowers growing among the grasses offer an ever-changing show of color. The display begins in April with the pasqueflower and continues until November when asters call "Halt" to the season.

One rainy day in mid-April Linda and I drove toward the

Loess Hills Wildlife Refuge in Monona County to look for pasque-flowers. It was Holy Saturday, the day before Easter, a most appropriate time to seek these symbols of spring's resurrection, which have been called the Easter plant. We began to drive the gravel roads in the hills in midmorning, and I became increasingly depressed at how some landowners were treating the land. Many slopes were barren and severely eroded because of overgrazing. There seemed to be a general absence of conservation-oriented farming practices. It was early spring and, at winter's end, vegetation was at a minimum. It appeared that the battle to save the hills was being lost.

We drove past the Loess Hills Wildlife Refuge, which had been recently burned and was as black as coal. In spite of its appearance we knew that fire is an integral and important part of prairie management. We turned a corner north of the refuge and I stopped to scan a grass-covered slope with binoculars. Instantly I saw the blue of pasqueflowers among tussocks of little bluestem. We soon discovered them over the entire slope and continued up the road to find the landowner. At the first driveway, Jerry Kessler, a potter and musician, warmly welcomed us and told us to walk his property wherever we wished.

Hundreds of pasqueflowers were growing a short distance up the slope. Because of the rain and overcast conditions, only a few had opened. The outside of an unopened flower is a pale blue which can go unnoticed when the flowers are open. The flowers, composed of five to seven sepals, lack true petals. They open only when there is adequate light and begin to close on sunny days shortly before sunset. The seed heads of pasqueflowers, which resemble miniature upturned feather dusters, disintegrate in the wind to scatter new progeny over the prairie.

In pouring rain we covered only a small portion of the slope but spent nearly three hours studying and photographing the flowers. Finding so many flowers was like a revelation that gave the resurrection a deeper meaning.

During late May and early June, the pervasive loco-weed colors hillsides magenta. Overgrazing where this plant is common can cause livestock poisoning. Affected animals become spooky, exhibit trembling and paralysis, and eventually die if they fail to find alternate food sources. In late spring and early summer, purple prairie clover and leadplant (both legumes), prairie larkspur (a white delphinium), and both prairie (yellow) and purple coneflowers weave their color among the flowing grasses of little bluestem and side-oats grama.

By midsummer, the stately stalks of the compass-plant overshadow the essentially leafless stems of skeleton weed (also called rush pink). Both plants were favorites of pioneer children, who used the compass-plant's resin and the skeleton weed's juice for chewing gum.

The warm, dry climate provides agreeable habitat for numerous plants normally found several hundred miles to the west and south. Besides skeleton weed and nineanther dalea, a notable plant growing far east of its normal range is yucca, or soapweed. Although similar to the common garden yucca, it is a different species. In June, glowing candles of flowers (hence the name, Lord's candle) rising above its dagger-like evergreen leaves mark the way toward summer.

One species new to science—the prairie moonwort—was discovered in 1982. It is a small, inconspicuous fern that grows on dry, open slopes or on the edge of the prairie under shrubs such as dogwood.

The Loess Hills area also supports wildlife commonly identified with western and southern states. Lizards found in the bluffs region but absent elsewhere in the state include the Great Plains skink and the prairie racerunner. The plains pocket mouse, Great Plains toad, Woodhouse's toad, plains spadefoot toad, and prairie rattlesnake are also east of their normal range.

West side of the Loess Hills formation with yucca, looking south from the top of Murray Hill, Harrison County.

More than 100 bird species likely nest in the hills. The Say's phoebe, burrowing owl, blue grosbeak, and western kingbird, which are all relatively uncommon or rare in Iowa, can be found on the Missouri River floodplain. Burrowing owls are often reported near Onawa, and western kingbirds are guaranteed in summer at the Sioux City airport. Savanna habitat of the loess foothills in Fremont and Mills counties is one of the best places to find the elusive chuck-will's-widow in Iowa. However, birder Larry Farmer once told me he heard its nighttime call on his farm in Plymouth County on the north edge of the loess range.

Raptor specialist Jon Stravers believes the Loess Hills may be an important midcontinental flyway for birds of prey. Species such as Krider's red-tail, the ferruginous hawk, Swainson's hawk, the golden eagle, and the prairie falcon can be seen during migration periods.

Great numbers of snow geese and other waterfowl use the Missouri River flyway; thus the distant hills often become part of the waterfowl spectacle. DeSoto National Wildlife Refuge, which includes the cut-off Missouri River oxbow known as DeSoto Bend, usually has several hundred thousand migrating snow geese as well as ducks in early and mid-November. They stay until freezing weather forces them south.

For much of the 160 miles from the Missouri line to Westfield in Plymouth County, secondary roads running along the base of the bluffs offer easy access to the foothills. From these baseline roads, numerous winding routes cross the Loess Hills. A particularly picturesque drive unfolds along County Road F-20 as it heads east from Little Sioux towards Pisgah in northern Harrison County. Next to a small public access, one can scale a high ridge known as Murray Hill for a spectacular view of the bluffs and the Missouri River valley.

In Harrison and Monona counties, the Loess Hills Pioneer State Forest includes 6,000 acres of a projected 17,000 acres when acquisition is completed. Primitive trails now give access to the rugged terrain.

*Autumn color of smooth sumac and native prairie grasses in northern
Loess Hills landscape at Stevenson Family Preserve, Plymouth County.*

Other places worth visiting include the forested valleys of Preparation Canyon State Park in Monona County and the Loess Hills Wildlife Refuge north of Turin, which comprises over 2,700 acres of forest, prairie, and farmland. Within this unit is the Turin Loess Hills State Preserve, a prime example of the loess topography where management goals are to establish optimum conditions for a diverse flora and fauna.

In the northern Loess Hills landscape the Iowa Chapter of The Nature Conservancy has protected four areas. Sioux City Prairie consists of 160 acres within the city limits. In Plymouth County three areas have been protected: Five Ridge Prairie at 790 acres; and Broken Kettle Grassland, consisting of the 640-acre Ryan tract and the 500-acre Stevenson Family Preserve. Although ownership of Five Ridge Prairie has been transferred to the Plymouth County Conservation Board, all areas are managed or jointly managed by The Nature Conservancy.

To the south, in Council Bluffs, at least two bluff-situated public areas provide scenic vistas: Lewis and Clark Monument is on the north edge of the city, and Fairmount Park is southwest of the downtown business district. Because loess is easily disturbed, these city parks need maintained trails to control foot traffic. Slopes must also be protected from off-road vehicles or the loose soil quickly erodes, starting new gullies. Waubonsie State Park in Fremont County, in the extreme southwest corner of the state, contains sheltered wooded valleys and open bluff faces that are accessible by an excellent system of hiking trails.

Although many areas are publicly owned, the greater part of the land covered by the Loess Hills remains in private hands. Continued efforts to protect significant portions and to educate Iowans about its unique features will guarantee the future existence of this fragile landform.

Frost-covered common cattails frozen in clear ice along the edge of a prairie pothole marsh at Anderson Lake, Hamilton County.

Prairie Marshes

Dusk nears as I begin my walk across the smooth slate-gray ice along the southern edge of Hendrickson Marsh in eastern Story County. There is a cold, damp northwest wind which cuts to the bone as it gusts, sweeping dried willow and cottonwood leaves across the open ice, hurling them end over end. In the approaching darkness, I hear the low rhythmic hoot of a great horned owl about to begin his evening forays.

Winter officially arrives in the marsh when the last patch of open water freezes and waterfowl no longer stop and linger. Winter marshes are not places of moderation. Bitter cold with a biting wind often follows calm and moderate weather. Life is seemingly absent in this harsh, forbidding, and silent world, yet activity continues beneath the insulating coat of ice. Water movement may be visible through the ice only when muskrats disturb the muddy bottom, searching for food cached before freeze-up. Frogs and turtles are buried beneath the muck, their metabolism near standstill. Vegetation appears to be in a state of carnage with the shattered remains of cattails, bulrushes, and phragmites everywhere. Most plant life is locked up in seeds and overwintering rootstocks, awaiting the spring warm-up.

Snow changes the character of the marsh as it begins to plummet earthward. It piles cap-like on grass heads, milkweed pods, and cattails until gravity or a wind gust causes it to tumble silently into white oblivion. One can begin to find evidence of resident meadow voles, deer mice, rabbits, and shrews in their trails.

If I can time my visit to the winter marsh when high icy cirrus clouds precede a front moving in from the west, the reward is a dramatic sunset. Ten to 20 minutes after the sun drops below the horizon, the color begins. Vivid yellows followed by orange, red, and finally magenta in slow progression paint the gradually darkening sky. Old, scraggly black willows become magnificent silhouettes, while slick, smooth ice mirrors the changing hues.

Ice-locked February marshes retain the winter quiet of January cold, giving no promise of spring. If severe cold prevails for extended periods of time, shallows of deep-water marshes and prairie potholes may freeze to the muck below. Muskrats may be cut off from cattail tubers and other underwater plants and forced to forage on the ice's surface, where they become easy prey for foxes, mink, hawks, and owls. Fish trapped by a freeze-out may gulp for air beneath the ice or simply die of oxygen deprivation. Ironically, mink may benefit from the devastation of a severe winter and feast on the remains well into early spring.

Days pass in the winter marsh, and life seems to pause. Unless dramatic weather occurs, one day appears very much like the next.

As weather systems move across the continent, the counterclockwise rotation of low pressure air masses often brings moisture-laden Gulf air up from the south. If the moist air meets a cold front or overrides a heavy snow cover, it may produce winter fog, a great source of rime frost. The buildup of frost continues hour after hour, crystal upon crystal until the snow, the sky, and land are nearly indistinguishable.

One winter night a thick fog forced me to drive home at a

Black willow branches frozen down on the edge of a prairie pothole marsh at Anderson Lake, Hamilton County.

snail's pace, my eyes glued to the centerline. The temperature was just below freezing, and before I arrived home, a layer of rime frost had formed on tree branches and powerlines. It was no time to be on the road, but the frost promised a dazzling sight come daybreak.

The following morning I arose before dawn and drove to the western edge of Hendrickson Marsh. The fog had dissipated, but throughout the night its soft brush-like strokes had coated cattails, grasses, and barren willows with thick layers of frost. Before sunrise the landscape reflected a tinge of blue from the clear morning sky, but when the first rays of the rising sun topped distant willows, each frost-covered object glowed as if it were producing its own light. As the sun rose, the gold patterns turned to silver and the facets of each crystal face liberated tiny suns.

The layers of frost had enlarged every blade and branch to many times its normal size. Since the day was windless, the white coating retained its perfection until midmorning. Ironically, the same warm rays which had lighted this glorious creation would also spell its doom. As melting progressed, white stems became tiny rivulets. Barren tree branches gradually lost their crystal leaves in a showering array and resumed somber winter stature. The awe-inspiring frosted landscape soon became a wet world of gray and brown grass, leaves, and branches.

Change in the winter marsh begins in late February or early March when prevailing winds switch to the southwest. Daylength has increased almost two hours since late December, and birds are eager to head north. Mallards, pintails, Canada geese, and common mergansers are often the first to arrive and sit on the ice or feed and bathe in patches of open water.

With the first warm-up, thick white ice turns gray and mushy and begins to melt in protected shallows. Wind action may hasten the initial breakup of ice. Warm spring weather is, however, not a foregone conclusion. On cold, calm mornings thin transparent sheets of clear ice often re-form. In a Story County prairie pothole, I

Rime frost on grasses and pussy willows in the south pond at Prairie Creek Wildlife Refuge, Marshall County.

once watched a group of ring-necks and bluebills feeding in broken shell-ice. The glass-like pieces chimed against one another as a brisk northwest wind piled them upon the shore.

In early March the weather can still be gray and overcast; snow squalls and weeks of cold weather are always a possibility. During one spring blizzard, my wife, Linda, and I watched hundreds of canvasbacks at Little Wall Lake in Hamilton County as driving snow reduced visibility to 100 feet. The "cans" just off shore seemed to take little note of the storm. They bobbed in the white caps, bathed, and dived for food. Weather to a canvasback is neither good nor bad.

Little Wall Lake was formerly a prairie marsh and is still a traditional stopover spot for thousands of waterfowl. In March the lake often refreezes after being entirely open. One afternoon in mid-March we observed about 10,000 birds on the lake. They extended along a narrow band of open water from southeast to northwest. In open water, great numbers of common mergansers, lesser scaups, and ring-necks were courting. Common golden-eyes carried on with much head extending and bobbing. A small group of shovelers fed with just part of their heads above water; huddled close together, head to tail, they turned in circles like whirligig beetles. There were also great blue herons, American widgeons, mallards, ring-billed gulls, and a small flock of buffleheads, which constantly flew about, then landed with five or six males pursuing a single female.

Later that same afternoon we drove a few miles north to Anderson Lake, a prairie pothole marsh maintained in its original condition by a sporting club. Filled with cattails and other emergent vegetation, it was at the "closed-in stage" of marsh succession. There was no open water, but several thousand mallards were sitting on the ice amongst the cattails. It was a very different scene from vegetation-free Little Wall only a few miles away. More ducks approached and landed as darkness settled in. The west was gray; there would be no sunset, so we headed for home.

Canvasback ducks during a spring blizzard in the open water of Little Wall Lake, Hamilton County.

One of the first birds to symbolize spring is the red-winged blackbird. Some may overwinter, but large flocks of males come in March to set up territories around marshes and along roadsides. In evening the noisy chorus heads for marshes to roost.

Yellow-headed blackbirds, unlike redwings, are strictly marsh dwellers. In central Iowa the earliest yellowheads arrive in early April. Late one afternoon I was photographing ducks when the weather turned cold and I found myself pushing a muskrat-house blind through rough open water into a bitter southeast wind. Four hours in chest-deep cold water not only had dampened my spirits but also had begun to impair my mobility. Just as I began to question the sanity of such undertakings, a bedlam of calls broke loose a few yards away. Swinging the blind around, I peered out to see six brilliant male yellow-headed blackbirds on cattails swaying wildly over the choppy water. Their boisterous proclamations seemed to defy adversity. As I glided closer, hoping for a photo-graph, they lifted, with white wing-patches blazing against the dark overcast, and turned leeward toward the cattail-choked northern shore. Their fleeting disappearance left me to battle the wind and waves, but the encounter sparked within me the warmth and needed energy to measurably shorten the last quarter mile to shore.

From our farmyard Linda and I are constantly reminded of prairie marshes. Just after the ice melts, we hear chorus frogs singing in a small prairie pond. It seems far too cold for amphibians to be moving about, let alone singing, but they announce spring with exuberance. The evening sky is often filled with small flocks of ducks that circle and "drop in" while we are eating supper. There are groups of mallards, scaups, ring-necks, blue-wings, and pairs of Canada geese. The most numerous bird, however, is the wood duck, which often funnels in well after sunset as darkness ap-proaches. Our pond is no more than an acre, yet they come in by the dozen. A bird that was almost lost is now abundant.

Entire days spent at a marsh can reveal far more than views

of ducks and geese. One mid-March morning I awoke at 4:00 A.M. to check the weather. Due south, the moon in its waning half glowed through a veil of cirrus. There was a cold, damp southwest wind, but the day would warm gradually as it progressed.

The eastern skyline had changed from a glow to mauve when I arrived on the west side of Hendrickson Marsh half an hour before sunrise. Gradually the sky turned red, then faded to deep orange. Against the changing hues, waterfowl silhouettes formed a constant parade. Streaming pintails, small flocks of teal, and mallard pairs moved about. Through the dry rattling reeds, I could hear the small talk of chuckling mallards and the occasional "quack! quack! quack!" from excited drakes.

Near the center of the marsh, a great gathering of snows and blues sat in the shallows along open water and on the ice. As the sun inched its way above the horizon, their restlessness increased. Minutes after sunrise they lifted with a thunderous roar of wings. Etched against the sky like Hitchcock's birds, they circled the marsh in an expanding black cloud, then headed into the wind and out to feed in long, disorderly waves. They would search the winter-weathered grainfields and likely return in late morning. Ducks also arose at the clamor, some headed for cornfields, others for shallows deep in the marsh. The airspace emptied as quickly as it had filled except for unsettled pairs of mallards and small flocks of teal.

By midmorning the geese had begun to return in long lop-sided V's that stretched to the horizon and beyond. In the shallow water, mallards and shovelers continued to dabble, while pairs of pintails courted, preened, whistled, and stirred up commotion among the other ducks. On an exposed mudflat, a muskrat began to feed, looking for fresh new greens. My continued presence finally drove him underwater, where he swam downstream to another exposed flat.

Intense quiet prevailed much of that afternoon until the resounding roll of a great rush of air told me the geese were up again.

I watched them rise, gradually gain altitude, and finally establish a heading due northwest. They did not disappear into the distance, however, and soon small groups began to return and kettle high above the marsh. Against the deep blue high overhead, they circled for nearly an hour, then settled down in open water on the far side of the marsh.

The tall grasses and cattails were brown, broken, and lodged in thick mats from winter snow. The marsh vegetation showed evidence of winter destruction everywhere, although fresh green shoots had begun to sprout along the incoming glade-like stream. As I crawled along a small embankment to prevent spooking birds on its far side, I sensed the musky smell of decaying vegetation. Humus formation was under way. I crossed a small channel beyond the dike, proceeded though a willow entanglement, and settled down in the shade on an old willow stump, draping myself with camouflage cloth. A chilly wind from the northeast wiped away the farm country sounds of central Iowa and brought solitude reminiscent of an old prairie marsh. In the distance, blue water met dry brown grasses that climbed the hillside unbroken to the skyline.

The old willow formed a rather narrow, hard seat, but I stopped thinking about it when a ball of brown fur bounded toward me, splashing through the shallow water. It was a mink; I whistled, hoping he would stop, while I tried to focus a cold, sluggish camera lens. He did not break his bounding stride, however, and soon was behind me, through the willows, and out of sight.

Forty feet from me, a large muskrat house loomed in the blue water. Between wind gusts I could hear the whimpering of young inside the lodge. Two hours passed, during which a stiff crosswind had developed and the cold had begun to penetrate. The ducks had failed to return in numbers, but sighting the mink had made the wait worthwhile.

As dusk settled in, sweeping cirrus clouds gave the prom–ise of a new weather front for the coming day. In open water, a

Snow geese silhouetted against the sky just after sunrise at Hendrickson Marsh, Story County.

sprinkling of ducks was surrounded by a small flock of Canada geese. Over the shallow water, descending swarms of mallards received reassuring chuckles from those feeding below. They came in from every direction as darkness overtook daylight.

In less than 20 minutes, the east was dark and the western sky had turned mauve. Old willows loomed ghost-like against pink water and sky. Sounds were those of ducks except for a faint honking that gradually grew in magnitude, foretelling the arrival of geese. Their honking became a constant din to serenade the oncoming darkness. Circling only once, they began to slip-slide down. Soft whistling sounds accompanied their fall as air rushed past oblique wings. Just above the water, wings parachuted open for landing.

Darkness had nearly enveloped the sky when a small squadron of teal sped overhead and disappeared into the eastern darkness. It was time to sit and listen. In the distance, high notes of white-fronts came out of nowhere, then faded into the soft nighttime music of the snows and blues.

Sugar maple and an old white oak in a cold autumn rain at Mossy Glen State Preserve, Clayton County.

Indian Summer's End

*I*ndian summer days occur between autumn's color extravaganza and winter's first snow. They never seem to last long enough, for with their gradual departure in late fall, cold northwest winds and overcast skies impart a sullen mood across the countryside. The gray-brown landscape is a sharp contrast from the vivid greens and blues of bright spring and summer days. Most people see early winter as dull, with monotonous hues and a lack of striking variation. Earth tones attract little attention though they are rich in pattern and design and sprinkled with bits of green, red, and yellow.

Streamside sycamores reveal a rich tapestry with their flaking chalk-white bark. The trunks of these grand trees on riverbanks stand out in sharp contrast to the dark browns of cottonwoods and the grays of silver maples. Sycamores have enormous palmately-lobed leaves which litter the landscape and shelter myriad microorganisms from the drying effects of wind and sunlight.

As I walk along a meandering creek I see the tattered ends of summer weariness at each bank and bend. Where rich green fields of sedge flourished a few weeks earlier, lodged brown stalks wait for matting snow. On the crest of a dirt bank, foxtail grass has turned a tawny yellow and its seed heads wave in the wind.

Near a bend in the creek, I disturb ground-feeding tree sparrows. They scurry ahead, alighting on broken branches and dried weed stalks. Like most fall sparrows, their primary colors are gray and brown, but they are by no means drab with their neat little rust-colored caps. They will soon be joined by dark-eyed juncos, which are generally gray, black, and white, although an occasional individual may have a brown head.

Along most small prairie streams, old eastern cottonwoods stand as sentinels. A tree of the lowlands, it has rough, deeply furrowed bark that glows, when wet, with bluish-gray, chartreuse, and green lichens. Beneath these old monarchs I watch the water flow. The lacework pattern of ice will soon decorate riffle areas with crystalline finery. Nearby, leafless branches and trunks of black willows appear stark and lifeless. I stop to inspect an amber willow wand; its tender little pointed buds lace up the stem. Each bud contains the embryo for new leaves and awaits the radiant warmth of spring. The buds remind me that timing is nature's key to life as the seasons advance.

Downstream, I come to a barbed wire fence which excludes cattle from an adjoining area. Its overgrown appearance presents a striking example of what happens when nature takes control. Without grazing or fire, natural succession turns most grasslands into woodlands.

As I prepare to cross the fence, the silhouette of a hovering hawk demands identification. My binoculars reveal he too is brown but has a white-tipped tail with a broad black band. Rough-legged hawks are winter residents commonly seen hovering as they hunt for prey. They will also scavenge if the opportunity arises.

In late autumn, prairies are a rich mosaic of somber colors. After an autumn rain, little bluestem on dry upper hillside slopes can appear rich auburn in color. Most of the tall grasses are still standing and can be difficult to wade through. The light yellow-brown of big bluestem, Indian grass, and switchgrass will gradually fade from the bleaching effects of winter rain, wind, snow, and sunlight. Intermingled with the prairie grasses are the dark heads of bushclover, woolly vervain, and a dozen sunflowers.

In a small pothole marsh, maroon stems of smartweed cover mud bars. Grayish-tan cattail stems are in tangled disarray, their seed heads tattered or barren. Slough grass, the purest yellow in autumn, gradually weathers into the muted tans of cattails and bulrushes. Milkweeds are a washed-out gray. Most of the horn-like pods have split wide; a few still contain seeds but most are only empty scabbards, their future progeny scattered about the countryside.

As I walk I hear twittering goldfinches. Their olive-brown winter plumage is highlighted by bright black and yellow, with white wing bars. They hop from the ragged remains of tall thistles to seed heads atop brittle stalks of giant ragweed. The black-capped chickadee also has the seeds of giant ragweed on its menu.

In early November, after a week of rain and cloudy weather, I take to the woods in search of mosses. Insect activity has been reduced for the most part to overwintering pupae, while migrating juncos seem to be discussing winter tenure. The mosses appear everywhere as phosphorescent green blotches in the forest woodwork. Fallen logs, tree bases, strips of broken bark, rocks, and exposed dirt banks glow with the velvet verdure. The green of mosses is far richer than in spring and easier to see than in summer, when leaves masked its color. It is invigorating to see thriving growth at the end of autumn—the exuberance of youth as winter begins.

Our vision of nature's subtle features is a mere matter of choice. The ability to see is dictated more by humble curiosity than by some acute vision. Most of us see only what we want to see, not necessarily the world before us. When the landscape's subtle intricacies pass us by, weeks and months are viewed as seasons without merit or opportunity. We have imprisoned ourselves in a thought process that dismisses today in the hope that tomorrow will shed light on what we regard as a dismal, lifeless landscape. Just a walk in the woods or through the fields can change our view and open our minds. Nature's renewal is always there.

Pennsylvanian-age sandstone covered with the moss Anomodon, *marginal shield ferns, and yellow birches along the Iowa River at Fallen Rock State Preserve, Hardin County.*

Juvenile red fox along a country road in Marshall County.

Critters

Most observers of wildlife in Iowa are birders or hunters. Collectively, bird watching by ordinary citizens has contributed immensely to our general understanding of the movements, distribution, and behavior of birds. Hunters observe mammals in the field, while the average person is more likely to encounter deer on the highway, raccoons in the garbage can, rabbits in the garden, or squirrels in the backyard. Few sightings are made of obscure species such as the short-tailed shrew, least weasel, or flying squirrel. Butterfly enthusiasts become more numerous each year, but there are not many hard-core lepidopterists. Even fewer individuals seek out reptiles and amphibians; only curious youngsters find the occasional garter snake or leopard frog.

A great diversity of animal life exists in Iowa's native habitats although these natural environments occupy only a fraction of their original area. Diversified agriculture can provide good wildlife habitat, but it is the exception today since the majority of farmers plant only corn and soybeans. Some species of wildlife, such as vesper sparrows and red-winged blackbirds, have adapted to intensive agricultural practices, but many more species exist only in isolated locations.

Before pioneer settlement, many mammals were active by day, but because of a long history of persecution, they have become nocturnal. Carnivores such as foxes and badgers, which are at the top of the food chain, can still be seen hunting during daylight on occasion, but they restrict most of their activities to the hours of darkness.

One of my favorite mammals is the red fox. We constantly hear that coyotes are out-competing red foxes for territory, but at no time in the past have I seen so much evidence of red foxes.

My opportunities to observe red foxes during daylight hours have been limited; thus I can remember nearly every sighting during the past 40 years. One autumn afternoon near Yellow River State Forest in northeast Iowa I watched a red fox hunting in a pasture along Paint Creek. He was completely unaware of my presence and went from one grass tussock to another seeking the scent of prey. He often stopped and pounced to flush or trap prey, which likely consisted of meadow voles, deer mice, or frogs. This is often called the "lunge and pin" method, a behavior we have all observed in the barnyard cat.

Red foxes are well adapted to the rigors of our mid-continental climate with its temperature extremes. One January night the wind howled out of the northwest and the temperature was well below zero Fahrenheit as I drove south of Clemons in western Marshall County. Near the crest of a high hill a running red fox entered the beams from my headlights. It was just a fleeting glimpse, but I can still see him heading into the knife-edge wind as if it did not exist. His body was so well furred it appeared almost round with an enormous white-tipped bushy tail extending straight back. I still marvel at his superb adaptation to cold, which made survival that frigid night just a walk-in-the-park.

Linda and I have spent many an evening watching young foxes near den sites in fields and along roadsides. As soon as youngsters emerge from the den, they begin to run about playing games, wrestling with one another, and pouncing on each other or some make-believe prey. In late May and early June they gradually begin to leave home, a process which occurs due to boredom and hunger as the parents bring less food to the den.

One such evening in early June we watched three juveniles for perhaps an hour. A month earlier we had seen what appeared to be active diggings along this road and decided to drive by them again. As we drove past, a flash of red caught my eye. I slowed to a halt and looked in my rearview mirror. I saw two pups near the den, so we turned around and drove cautiously back up the road.

At first the pups dove into the den, but in moments they were back out watching us. Soon they began to move about and ran to the top of the roadcut, then back down through the ditch and up onto the road. Fortunately there was little traffic. Two of the three were in a constant state of motion, nuzzling each other and rolling about. The third pup seemed more cautious and spent most of its time watching us, although it occasionally got caught up in the activity of its siblings. Constant activity prevailed for about 45 minutes, then two of the pups disappeared. Finally, we saw the third one move down the fence line and head across a cornfield. We could barely keep track of it in the approaching darkness.

As we drove on, Linda soon spotted one of the foxes in the distance crossing an open field toward a rise nearly half a mile away. At first we were baffled by their disappearance, but then we could see five fox silhouettes against a darkening skyline. The youngsters were with their parents, frolicking about. Perhaps the parents had called them away? Although we could not know for sure, they would probably never spend another night at their den site. For us it had been an eventful evening going home from the grocery store.

At another roadside den, there were also three young foxes at the end of the first week in June. Much activity was evident around the den site. Three major holes 15 feet apart entered the bank about two feet below its crest. The vegetation on the road bank was well worn with trails that led from one entrance to another. The fox pups seemed to prefer the left-most opening but went down all of them on occasion. Activity was almost nonstop among the three as they played. It is play with a purpose, as they hone their skills for survival by wrestling, chasing, and pouncing upon each other. One youngster often stopped to chew on a large old bone and aggressively defended it. They would often stretch out, with their front feet extended and rear quarters elevated, and yawn. At times the pace of the activity was difficult to follow. They ran in and out of the den holes and up, down, and over the road bank. As darkness descended, the activity level increased. We continued to watch them until half an hour past sunset, when it became difficult to see and their pace of activity slowed.

Badgers occupy habitats similar to those of foxes. In the mid-1970s I began to look for them and frequently stopped to explore roadside diggings. I soon learned that when badgers seek their prey, they often make a number of exploratory diggings to get a fix on the location of their prey before they actually dig it out. I also learned that the earth inside the top of badger holes usually shows the long scratch marks made by their front claws. My goal was to observe and photograph a badger, but first I needed to locate an active animal near its den.

One afternoon I stopped along a gravel road north of State Center in western Marshall County to check an area where there were fresh diggings. Peering down the largest hole, I caught sight of movement and glimpsed a white face as a hissing snarl came my way. As I retreated from the bank I removed some grass that obstructed the entrance and moved my truck directly across the road to watch. In less than a minute, a badger peered out, then immediately retreated by backing down the hole. After two and a half hours with no sign of activity, I headed home for supper. I returned about 6:50 P.M. Thirty seconds after I stopped the car a badger head

Badger atop his mound along a country road in western Marshall County.

Thirteen-lined ground squirrel with a gray partridge egg at Stinson Prairie, Kossuth County.

appeared and was looking my way. He climbed onto the top of his mound, put his head down between his paws, and started to doze in the sun. I was able to take numerous photos without disturbing him. About 7:00 P.M. he got up, turned around, and went down the hole headfirst. At 7:01 he reappeared, looked around momentarily, then lay down on the mound, draping himself over the hump of dirt at its entrance, and gradually closed his eyes. As a car approached ten minutes later, he got up, looked down the road, then headed down his hole as it passed. In a few minutes he was back out lying across the top of the mound—looking like an extra thick pancake—dozing in the sun. As my friend Darrell Norman arrived to observe, the badger again disappeared but came up momentarily and lay down as before. This behavior was repeated several more times until shadows fell across the entrance of the den at about 7:45, when he went down his hole and did not reappear. I was able to use up nearly all the film in my camera. It was a momentous occasion after more than a year of searching and waiting.

Thirteen-lined ground squirrels, an important prey species for the badger and red fox, are abundant throughout Iowa. They are found in the short grass along most roadsides and in golf courses, lawns, overgrazed pastures, and treeless cemeteries. Since they hibernate, we often see them the last time in mid- to late November, then not again until mid- to late March. On December 9, 1990, we were driving near home when we saw one along the shoulder of the road. He ran across 10 inches of snow in the ditch and entered a hole in the snow. The forecast was for temperatures in the 50s, so perhaps he knew there was warm weather ahead.

One of our most interesting observations occurred at Stinson Prairie State Preserve in Kossuth County. It was March and we had walked over much of the prairie looking for pasqueflowers when we spotted a thirteen-lined ground squirrel rolling a gray partridge egg about. He tried to gain access to its contents, but the egg was just too big to crush in his jaws. The shell was slick and smooth, and he could not get his teeth to break through the surface. While I am basically against interfering, I wanted to see what would happen if this squirrel gained access to the contents of the egg, so I entered the scene and cracked the shell ever so slightly. We waited for his return, and in a matter of seconds he had the egg open and was relishing its contents. Like most other mammals, ground squirrels are opportunistic.

Three species of tree squirrels are found in Iowa—the fox squirrel, the gray squirrel, and the red squirrel. Fox squirrels are quite evenly distributed throughout the state. Gray squirrels are most common in the eastern part of the state. Red squirrels are found from Forest City to the Mississippi River down to Cedar Falls.

Fox squirrels are found in cities and in the countryside, even where the timber is quite marginal. Birders often consider them a nuisance; however, they are responsible for planting native woodland because they bury seasonal supplies of acorns, hickories, and walnuts. A black, or melanistic, phase of the fox squirrel can be found along both the Mississippi and Missouri rivers. I have seen them in Davenport, in the Loess Hills, and at DeSoto National Wildlife Refuge. If the light is right, the copper red typical of fox squirrels can be seen in their fur.

Because squirrels are often front yard residents, they offer us prime opportunities to observe their behavior. In late winter, fox squirrels in our farmyard cut dry red oak leaves off a small tree across our lane and carry them to their nest holes to prepare for a new litter of young. It is a time-consuming process when only a few leaves can be carried at a time. We have also seen fox squirrels gnaw the bark from sugar maple branches in March to start the sap flowing, then, while hanging upside down, drink the liquid from the wound. Often cedar waxwings hover beneath the same branches to catch the dripping sap.

Mink have always been residents of our farm and can be seen on occasion along streams, rivers, and lakes. (If a person

Western chorus frog along the Iowa River, Marshall County.

stands still after sighting a mink, it will often go about its business as if the observer did not exist.) I have seen them hunting in midday along the edge of our farm creek; they favor undercut banks where there are overhanging roots. One had a den site beneath an old silver maple, and I could count on seeing him nearby with regularity.

I have also seen mink far from water. One summer afternoon I spotted one next to our garage near a flowerbed that is nearly half a mile from the creek. One year we lost nearly all our baby chickens to an unknown critter. Could it have been a mink?

On a frigid morning in March I was driving around Storm Lake in Buena Vista County when I spotted a mink on the ice in a small cove. He explored dead grass, rocks, and old roots until he came to a small opening in the ice, where he dove beneath the surface. After a very short time, he reappeared and headed off down the shoreline. Was he hoping to find a fish? As with many observations of wildlife, we are left with more questions than answers.

Gray treefrogs and western chorus frogs are common over much of Iowa but are not often seen because of their small size. The gray treefrog has a bird-like call that can be dismissed as "just another bird" when it is heard singing in the trees overhead. After a person learns its call, gray treefrogs appear to be practically everywhere. Several summers ago one sat on my office windowsill, which is directly above a bed of ostrich ferns, and announced his presence with song throughout the day. During the summer of 1992 a gray treefrog came to Linda's upstairs office window each evening for several weeks. Since our indoor lighting attracted many insects, he found it an excellent foraging ground for large moths. During daylight hours we searched for him but never did discover his hiding place.

When one begins to notice wildlife, first observations, are often viewed as rare sightings even though they are commonplace events. On occasion, however, what one considers to be common-

White-lipped triodopsis in mature sugar maple forest, Clayton County.

place may, in fact, be a rare occurrence. During the summer of 1976 Larry Stone and I were exploring a northeast Iowa woods. It was a moist, damp day after an August rain and a chorus of gray treefrogs kept us searching for them. We finally found one which blended perfectly with the lichen-covered bark 10 feet from the ground in a small tree.

Throughout the woods were large land snails known as white-lipped triodopsis. We found them on fallen leaves and on the roots and trunks of trees. They appeared to be as abundant as robins in spring migration. In all the years since, I have seen only a few living specimens, although I occasionally find empty snail shells in woodland leaf litter.

Insect observations can involve seasons of effort and just plain luck. On occasion I have found cecropia and polyphemus moths clinging to branches or shrubbery in midday. More frequently I have found the larval caterpillar stage, and in the interest of obtaining photos of a perfect specimen, I have kept them over the winter to watch the adults emerge in the spring.

My first experience, however, was full of surprises. Quite by accident I found a cecropia moth larva crawling across our front yard in September. I put it in a pail of fresh leaves, where it cocooned, and left it on an open-air porch to overwinter. In late winter I scheduled a trip to the Southwest to photograph desert flowers. Since I wanted to be sure to see the adult emerge, I put the chrysalis in our deep freeze until I returned home. I then tied it to the back of a lawn chair on our screened porch and proceeded to wait. Weeks passed, and I began to wonder it if would hatch. Had it been parasitized? Did the stint in our freezer cause complications?

In late June we headed for a small-town parade and took the lawn chairs along, forgetting that the chrysalis was tied to the back of one of them. Upon our arrival, the lawn chairs were deemed unnecessary and were left in the car. Several hours had passed when we returned to our vehicle to find a fully formed cecropia moth

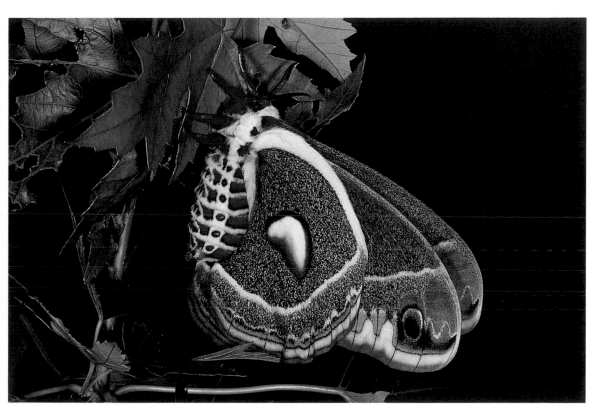

Cecropia moth at Prairie Creek Wildlife Refuge, Marshall County.

fluttering against the closed windows. That evening I photographed it successfully and, in darkness, released it to find a mate, lay eggs, and propagate its species.

Deer mice, meadow voles, short-tailed shrews, and least shrews can occupy diversified farmland in large numbers. We have often captured them and kept them in captivity to photograph them and to study their behavior. Mice and voles are rodents and thus are easy to feed and care for, whereas shrews require a live diet such as insects or earthworms (although I have read accounts of them living on carrion). One October we kept a short-tailed shrew for nearly a month. It was during harvest season, and each night after a day in the field, we found ourselves digging worms by flashlight to feed a voracious shrew. We finally photographed and released him. Within seconds he disappeared beneath the leaf litter on the edge of our woods.

The opportunities to observe nature's best moments often occur when and where we least expect them. They enlarge our world whether we are at home, on a city street, or in the finest natural area.

Sugar maples in mixed deciduous forest at Fort Defiance State Park, Emmet County.

Native Woodlands

Pioneers traveling westward were greeted by a strange new land as they entered Iowa from its bordering rivers. As far as the eye could see, treeless rolling hills ruled the landscape except for occasional cottonwood stands along stream bottoms and a few forested river valleys. The open country was virgin tallgrass prairie that stretched to the horizon and was open to the sun and the sky. The sea of grass had not only maintained itself for thousands of years but also had built beneath its turf some of the world's richest soil. It was a land far removed from tall, dense eastern forest.

The first pioneers were unfamiliar with grasslands and reasoned that if the land was too poor to grow trees, it must also be too poor to grow crops. Thus those who came first often settled within woodlands similar to the eastern forest they had left behind.

The woods provided many of the necessities that the open prairie lacked. They offered protection from the ever-blowing wind, wood for building barns and homes, fuel for heat, abundant game for food, and adequate stream water for home use and for watering livestock. Because the early settlers preferred woods over prairie, woodlands sold for five to 10 times more per acre than native

Serviceberry in red oak woods along the north shore of Lower Pine Lake at Pine Lake State Park, Hardin County.

prairie in central Iowa in the 1860s. Today many Iowa farms are still nestled within the trees of native woods, but the value of open prairie turned to farmland has far outstripped that of timberland.

The greatest concentrations of original woodlands were in the rough unglaciated northeast; along the corridors of the Mississippi and Missouri rivers; in valleys of southeast and south central Iowa; and in corridors along larger interior streams and rivers—areas which today are commonly called "greenbelts."

Only 19 percent of Iowa's 35.8 million acres of land was originally forested. About 5 percent remains. Every county in the state has some forestland, but the amount varies from 32 percent in Allamakee County to less than 1 percent in Grundy and Pocahontas counties. Farmers own about 90 percent of the total wooded land in the state.

Iowa forests have 76 species of native trees. Most are hardwoods, that is, broad-leafed trees, though small scattered stands of softwoods, which are usually referred to as conifers or evergreens, can be found. Most tree species tend to grow in specific locations or sites; they are often found in association with other species which have similar habitat requirements. These groups of trees and associated herbaceous plants form a "community."

Oak-hickory forest, a common community type throughout Iowa, generally occurs on dry ridges and warm south- and west-facing slopes. The dominant trees are white oak and shagbark hickory, with black oak becoming common in the southeast. These woodlands have the occasional black cherry, which has dark reddish wood that is used to make fine furniture. The understory is usually ironwood—sometimes called American hophornbeam—a small, extremely shade-tolerant tree. Its wood, which, as the name implies, is as hard and strong as iron, is still used for tool handles. On the edge of these woods, we find smooth and staghorn sumac. Where there has been disturbance such as grazing, gooseberry and black raspberry bushes may become abundant.

Maple-basswood forest generally occurs on slopes which face north or east. These woodlands are more moist and cooler than oak-hickory communities. The dominant trees are black and sugar maples, northern red oaks, and basswoods (also known as American lindens). In dry upper slopes of some maple-basswood forest, red oaks are the dominant tree; they may form a high canopy, usually called the first canopy, above a second canopy of mature black and sugar maples. This cathedral-like forest does not likely develop in less than 200 years; thus where logging has occurred in the past century, the dominant trees are often sugar and black maples. These form a very tight, light-excluding leaf canopy which makes it difficult for other tree species to gain a foothold.

On moist north-facing slopes, sugar maple, basswood, and red oak co-dominate. Understory trees or secondary growth are mainly red oak, chinkapin oak, blue beech, basswood, and sugar maple. One of Iowa's most dramatic flowering trees occurs in the understory or at the boundary between oak-hickory and maple-basswood communities. Serviceberry, or shadbush, with clusters of white flowers that bloom in the early spring woods, is the "dog-wood" of the north. In late April hundreds of serviceberries officially announce the arrival of spring along the shoreline of Lower Pine Lake in Hardin County.

Bottomland or floodplain communities are characterized by plants which grow rapidly following disturbance such as stream meandering. If the soils of these woods are frequently waterlogged, they often support eastern cottonwood, boxelder, silver maple, black willow, and river birch. From central Iowa south and east along most rivers and streams, the American sycamore is also an increasingly common tree. Its chalky white bark stands out dramatically in the fall, winter, and spring when its broad "maple-shaped" leaves are absent. In far southeast Iowa, pin oaks grow with spreading buttresses on lowlands and floodplains. Many fine examples are found in Des Moines County and along the Mississippi River from

American sycamore along the floodplain of the Skunk River, Story County.

Muscatine south. River birches, as the name implies, grow on flood-plains throughout eastern Iowa. They are even on the edge of marshes such as Sweet Marsh near Tripoli in Bremer County. South of Clinton I have seen floodplains, once cleared for farming, come back to solid river birch stands a person could barely walk through. The understory of many floodplains can be a tangle of Virginia creeper, wild grape, and poison ivy. On some Mississippi River floodplains, poison ivy forms a dense wall taller than a man that is virtually impenetrable during summer months. In the absence of disturbance, bottomland communities may eventually be replaced by maple-basswood forest.

For a period of about 2,000 years following the retreat of the Wisconsin ice sheet into what is now Minnesota, Iowa's landscape was dominated by coniferous forest. Remnants of this boreal forest remain as pockets from central Iowa eastward on shaded north-facing slopes. The dominant trees are eastern white pine, balsam fir, sugar maple, paper birch, and yellow birch. The pines and firs are easiest to see in autumn when they stand out dramatically against the red and yellows of oaks and maples. Paper birches may also be mixed with quaking and big-tooth aspens on north-facing slopes and ridges. White pine, balsam fir, and eastern redcedar are Iowa's only native conifers except for Canada yew and common juniper, which are shrubs.

Eastern white pines, with their towering crowns, are among Iowa's most majestic trees; native stands are common along some river and stream valleys in northeast Iowa. Backbone State Park in Delaware County, Yellow River State Forest in Allamakee County, and White Pine Hollow State Preserve in Dubuque County contain many fine white pines.

White Pine Hollow State Preserve is a forest where the tall spires of old white pines predominate above the deciduous forest canopy. Lying in the northwest corner of Dubuque County, White Pine Hollow Forest Reserve was set aside by the State Conservation

Commission in about 1937, with the original purchase comprising 610 acres. Additional acres were added in 1942 and 1964, for a current total of 712 acres. In September 1968, the area was given State Preserve status, and in October 1972, it was made a National Natural Landmark. In his study of the region, Robert F. Thorne commented, "I know of no comparable square mile area in Iowa that can approach the reserve in the richness of its flora." Plant surveys by botanists at the University of Iowa have catalogued more than 625 species. Lying far south of similar coniferous forests in the north woods of Wisconsin, Minnesota, and southern Canada, White Pine Hollow is Iowa's best boreal forest relict. The cold, damp conditions of a characteristic boreal forest are duplicated on its steep, shaded slopes where water oozes from rock crevices. Other natural stands of eastern white pine are restricted to the Iowa River valley and Pine Lake State Park in Hardin County, and at Wildcat Den State Park in Muscatine County.

Balsam fir is found only in northeast Iowa, where the best natural stands are preserved along north-facing bluffs of the Upper Iowa and the Yellow rivers. Their pointed spires are especially attractive when mixed with paper birch trunks.

Eastern redcedar, a juniper rather than a true cedar, is not a member of the boreal forest. At home in openings within the broadleafed forests of the central United States, it is found throughout Iowa. Its tiny blue seeds are a favorite food for many birds, which are then correspondingly responsible for its widespread distribution. It quickly invades open areas such as prairies; since prairie fires are no longer a threat, redcedar is far more abundant that at any time in the past.

The trees of Iowa woodlands not only provide prime wildlife habitat and sustained yields of lumber, they also record environmental events with precision. We have all seen tree rings on a cutoff stump; they form because of the different growth rates and densities of springwood and summerwood. Springwood consists of

Paper birches, balsam firs, and a single eastern wahoo on a steep north-facing slope viewed across the Yellow River at Mountain Maple Hollow, Allamakee County.

broad, thin-walled cells, while the cells of summerwood are narrow and thick-walled. Thus rings in Iowa's oldest trees form a record of the past. Almost everyone has counted tree rings on a stump to age a tree, yet few know that the distance between each ring indicates annual moisture. Thus a storehouse of climatic information is locked up between the rings of trees.

The study of tree rings is known as dendrochronology. The word itself comes from the Greek word *dendron*, for "tree," and from *chronology*, the science of measuring time and dating events. In 1973, Dr. Roger Landers, an Iowa State University botanist, began a statewide study of tree rings. Cross sections from stumps are ideal for tree-ring dating, but Landers used only cross sections cut from dead trees. On living trees, he extracted a small pencil-size core from the trunk with a special coring tool that left the tree unharmed.

Landers found that redcedar and white pine growing on steep, rocky slopes where there is little soil or groundwater generally contained the best ring patterns for study because trees in these sites are the most sensitive to annual precipitation. Obtaining samples often required strenuous hiking or climbing high rock ledges. On many occasions I accompanied him in his search for old trees throughout the state. I was interested in forest ecology, and I also acted as a second person "safety net" in case of an accident. One day we were working in White Pine Hollow when he spotted an old redcedar stump dangling precariously from an inaccessible limestone ledge. I asked Jake, as his friends know him, how he planned to get it, and he jokingly replied, "I'll have to come back with a graduate student and a rope. After all, graduate students are expendable."

Fieldwork is usually the most enjoyable part of any research project, for after data has been gathered, the necessary and tedious lab work begins. Cross sections from tree stumps can be sanded and analyzed immediately, but cores the size of a lead pencil are quite fragile and need to be glued onto supports before they can be sanded smooth so the rings can be studied with a low-power microscope.

To establish a tree-ring chronology, the distance between rings is measured, then recorded on a graph. The pattern and frequency of wide and narrow rings makes it possible to cross-date living and dead material. This is the most important aspect of dendrochronology. If the ring pattern of a dead tree overlaps and matches up with the ring pattern of a living tree, one can go backward in time and extend the records of past climatic history beyond those contained in living trees.

In the mountains of the Southwest from Colorado to California, living bristlecone pines which are 4,600 years old have been cross-dated with dead material to establish continuous records that go back more than 8,000 years. Obviously, this is not possible in Iowa when the oldest living tree, a redcedar along the Cedar River in eastern Iowa found by Dr. Delores Graf of Iowa Wesleyan College, was but 450 years old in 1976. It is possible, however, that Iowa's climatic history can be extended back 1,000 years by cross-dating Iowa's oldest trees with dead wood from American Indian dwellings.

The relationship of tree-ring widths to weather could benefit Iowa's agricultural community. Because current Iowa weather records date back only 120 years, forecasters lack long-term weather data needed to predict trends. Data from tree-ring research might tell us how general past droughts have been and with what frequency they are likely to recur. Some insight might also be gained on the duration of droughts and the direction in which they travel.

Tree-ring studies have also been applied to other fields. Erosion rates and the frequency of floods can be determined by analysis of carefully selected trees. In archeology, old beams and charcoal from American Indian dwellings can be dated with precision by using tree-ring chronology, and the cost is far less than using the radioactive carbon-14 method. Environmental damage also can be seen in tree rings of certain species, since tree growth is often impaired where air pollution has been extensive.

In the southwestern desert, dendrochronology—which evolved as a science more than 70 years ago—still tells us more about the past than the future. However, with the use of computers and x-ray analysis of samples, Iowa's oldest living redcedars and white pines may be the prophets of our environmental future.

Iowa has no bristlecone pines or vast wilderness tracts, yet fine examples of native woodlands exist throughout the state. We can experience peaceful solitude on a walk in the woods and see natural succession as new trees sprout next to rotting logs. There is no haste, no urgency; renewal is everywhere, and nothing is wasted.

Rough blazing-stars and goldenrods on the slope of the glacial kettle at Freda Haffner Preserve, Dickinson County.

Big Kettle

Gentle slopes of original prairie landscapes were not just
featureless plains. Their flowing forms stretched away from
streams to uplands in undulating swells that rose and fell,
one beyond the other, until they were lost in the lights and shadows
of distant horizons.

Expanses of prairie survived longest in northwest Iowa,
where vistas similar to those the pioneers experienced can still be
seen. West of West Lake Okoboji in Dickinson County a unique
prairie landform known as a kettlehole has been preserved for
casual visitors and students of botany and geology. This has been
accomplished through the efforts of Iowa's chapter of The Nature
Conservancy and the generosity of the late Freda Haffner of
Burlington. Upon her death in 1969, Miss Haffner left a bequest to
the Conservancy for an Iowa project. In 1974 this money was used
to purchase Arend's Kettlehole and the surrounding 110 acres. This
entire site is now known as the Freda Haffner Preserve. Freda
Haffner would have found the botanical treasures of Big Kettle, as it
is often called, a never-ending source of pleasure, for it has been
said that her knowledge of unique plants extended over three counties near her home.

Big Kettle, a deep prairie pothole on the edge of the Little Sioux River floodplain, is surrounded by gently rolling land. Its formation involved a complex series of geologic processes that is fairly well understood, although certain aspects are still in question.

During the past 2 million years, several glacial epochs have shaped and reshaped Iowa's landscape. The last of these, known as the Wisconsin, advanced into the state about 14,000 years ago. This episode lasted only about 1,500 years. Two surges in the advance of ice, the Bemis and the Altamont, played a major role in forming Big Kettle.

Bemis ice came first, covering the land with perhaps hundreds of feet of ice. Generally, stagnant glaciers melt across their tops and along their leading edges and from beneath; in so doing, they form braided meltwater streams and leave knobby moraines, or hills, of glacial debris. In the case of the Bemis ice advance, meltwater, flowing beneath the glacier where the Little Sioux River presently flows, cut deep into the older glacial drift beneath. After the Bemis ice retreated, the Little Sioux flowed in a large trough.

The Altamont ice advance again filled the Little Sioux River valley, this time pushing a few miles farther west than the Bemis ice and thus breaking through the surging Bemis end moraine. Beneath the Altamont ice in the vicinity of the valley, meltwater flowed through small tunnels which grew in size as the water flow increased. These sub-glacial streams deposited sand and gravel, which later became ridges known as eskers. As the Altamont ice continued to melt, a large block of ice separated from the main ice mass and was surrounded by meltwater deposits. The melting of the ice block created the form of Big Kettle, a deep, quarter-mile-wide depression completely surrounded by glacial drift, especially sand and gravel.

Geologists call these phenomena "ice-contact" landforms. While there are few esker formations in Iowa, kettles persist throughout the region that was last covered by glaciers.

In 1899, T. H. Macbride vividly described the area in an Iowa Geological Survey report: "The topography of the region before us, for a prairie district, is remarkably varied; we have high mountain-like hills and ridges, long winding insignificant rivers (some in valleys extremely wide, others hemmed in by precipitous hills)." About the land northwest of Big Kettle, he said, "The hills simply defy classification or description. They pitch toward every point of the compass, they are of every height and shape, they rise by gradual ascent and fall off by precipices so steep that the most venturesome animal would scarcely attempt descent; they enclose high tablelands, wide low valleys that open nowhere; they carry lakes on their summits and undrained marshes at their feet; their gentle slopes are beautiful prairies easily amenable to the plough, their crowns are often beds of gravel capped with boulders and reefs of driven sand."

The bottom of Big Kettle was initially as low or lower in elevation than today's Little Sioux River, but erosion has partially filled it with sediments. Within these sediments lies a complete record of their deposition and of the botanical history of the area since the ice block melted.

During a survey of Big Kettle for the State Preserves Board in 1969, cores of the sediments were taken to a depth of 23 feet beneath the present marsh. Analysis of pollen within the peat and muck determined that lower levels were formed during a period of coniferous forest cover that followed rapid initial erosion when the land was barren.

Between 11,000 and 8,000 years ago, Iowa's climate gradually became warmer and drier. Because of this climate change, the coniferous forest of white and black spruce, tamarack, and balsam fir gave way to deciduous forest, which eventually yielded to prairie. During establishment of the prairie, a period of rapid erosion again covered the marsh with a layer of silts and sands. After prairie plants established themselves firmly on the steep slopes, erosion again subsided and a second layer of peat and muck began to form.

When the land now comprising Freda Haffner Preserve was acquired in 1974, the hill slopes and kettle had undergone a long history of cattle grazing. Roger Landers and I first visited the area one summer in the early 1970s. Prairie plants on the dry uplands were difficult to identify, since most were no more than a few inches in height. They were bonsais, so to speak, but still hanging on. There was also a clearly visible cattle trail extending from the southeast corner of the kettle, down into the bowl, and out over the rim at its lowest point on the west side. By the early 1990s, the prairie plant community had recovered beyond my wildest expectations—even the cattle trail was just barely visible. Nearly 55 acres of the 110-acre area had been cultivated when it was acquired by The Nature Conservancy in 1974. Since 1992, efforts have been under way to reconstruct a native prairie plant community on the previously farmed portion by using seed sources from the preserve and from Cayler Prairie, a few miles to the northwest. This will dramatically increase the area's viability as a refuge for both plant and animal life.

In 1976 Ed Crocker and I drove to the preserve in early April. Water in the kettle was cobalt blue under the clear morning sky and appeared to be deep, covering the emergent vegetation. On the dry rim, there was a profusion of pasqueflowers poking up through the dry remains of blue grama and hairy grama. The air was cold with a stiff southwest wind, but the promises of spring were at our feet. As we descended a steep hill on our return trip to Storm Lake, Ed suddenly turned the car off the road into a muddy ditch. We came to an immediate sinking halt, and he announced that there were no brakes.

Preliminary research of the modern flora of Big Kettle has revealed more than 300 species of plants within the preserve's boundaries. After pasqueflowers announce a new season, few new species bloom until mid-May, when the warmth of late spring beckons us

Long-plumed purple avens in evening light at Cayler Prairie State Preserve, Dickinson County.

to go for long walks. As on most other prairies, we can find orange phlox-like blossoms of hoary puccoon, pinks and whites of downy phlox, lavenders of loco-weed, tiny sunflowers of golden ragwort, and demure blossoms of blue-eyed grass.

In early June, long-plumed purple avens waves in the wind on the upper slopes and ridgetops. It is sometimes called prairie smoke or old man's beard, since plumes attached to the seed head remind one of a miniature feather duster.

The prairie celebration gets into full swing during late June and early July. Black-eyed Susans, purple coneflowers, purple prairie clover, and butterfly milkweed add bursts of color amid a flowing sea of porcupine grass (also called needlegrass). This cool-season grass grows in spring and drops its seed, which is needle-tipped with a long awn, in early summer. Alternating periods of moisture and dryness corkscrew the seed into the ground.

In late July and August, warm-season grasses such as little bluestem and side-oats grama begin to flower. On dry slopes they intermingle with the striking magentas of rough and dotted blazing-stars. When there is adequate moisture, their long flower spikes put on a dramatic show during mid-August.

Many species of sunflowers, asters, and goldenrods flower in September and early October.

To experience Big Kettle—especially its size—you must walk around the gravel rim where an occasional boulder outcrop or badger digging gives you cause to watch your step. Just after dawn and before dusk, when the shadows are long, you can best perceive the depth and breath of this enormous bowl. I always feel keenly insignificant against its backdrop, yet it is often in such a place that we become acutely aware of our own time and place.

*Female northern flicker and juvenile male at their nest cavity in an old
dead American elm at Prairie Creek Wildlife Refuge, Marshall County.*

Nesting

Spring brings the greatest number and variety of birds to
Iowa. Many species pass through the state and can be seen
for only a day or two, while others arrive to begin their nesting season here. More than 380 species of birds have been seen in
Iowa, but only about 150 species regularly nest in the state.

Bird nests are of a superb natural design. The nest may be a
simple cup or a hanging basket, although the common nighthawk
makes no nest at all. Most bird nests are symmetrical in shape and
are designed to contain the incubating parent, even if, as in the case
of the killdeer, the nest is only a depression in the ground. Some
nests, such as those of the oriole, red-winged blackbird, and robin,
are extremely well constructed and may persist long after the nesting season, while the nests of mourning doves, cardinals, and rose-
breasted grosbeaks barely make it through a single nest cycle. The
long, slender beaks of northern orioles and red-winged blackbirds
are well suited to the intricate weaving of grass, while the conical
bills of finches, such as cardinals, are poorly suited for nest con-
struction.

Each nest is designed to meet the needs of a particular
species, and birds make use of a wide variety of building materials.

A robin's nest consists of grass and is lined with a mixture of mud and fine grass, while a hummingbird's nest is constructed of plant down, fibers, and bud scales, covered with lichens, and attached to a limb with spider silk. The red-eyed vireo also attaches its nest with spider silk; the nest is hidden among leaves near the ends of long branches.

Many species in addition to robins incorporate mud into their nests. Barn swallows use a large percentage of mud to bind and attach grass and straw to chosen nest sites. Large colonies of cliff swallows plaster their jug-like nests, which are made entirely of mud or clay, to bridge supports, rocky cliffs, and occasionally the sides of buildings.

Chimney swifts are also quick to utilize human structures, as their name implies. Their nests of twigs are glued together and to the inside wall of a chimney or silo by using their own glutinous saliva, which eventually hardens.

Belted kingfishers and bank swallows tunnel into dirt, sand, or gravel banks and excavate burrows. In the case of the kingfisher the tunnels may be 6 to 10 feet long.

Old nests of one bird are sometimes taken over and modified by another. Great horned owls may use the abandoned nests of crows, hawks, or other large birds. They will also use squirrel nests, seek tree cavities, or even nest on natural rock ledges. Great-crested flycatchers and bluebirds seek natural tree cavities that were constructed by flickers, red-bellied woodpeckers, or red-headed woodpeckers in a previous year. Chickadees and titmice favor old nest sites by a bird more their size, the downy woodpecker.

Hummingbird nests are among the smallest in size, while eagle nests are huge, bulky structures. The nest of a bald eagle may contain many large branches and cornstalks (where they are available) in its base and be lined with twigs, grasses, and moss. Eagles' nests, normally about five feet across and two to three feet deep, are located in the tops of large old trees. Eagles often use the same nest

Red-eyed vireo with a butterfly chrysalis at its nest on the branch of a silver maple in a farm grove, Story County.

*Nest and eggs of a brown thrasher in a gooseberry at Illinois Grove,
Marshall County.*

year after year, adding new materials each nesting season. One of the largest known nests weighed two tons.

Most eggs are asymmetrical, which may keep them from rolling about, while others are nearly round. The eggs of birds that nest in tree holes or cavities usually are white and often are round, while the eggs of species that nest in the open have protective coloration and generally are asymmetrical. Some eggs are solid colors, others are mottled or speckled, and many incorporate a combination of patterns and designs unique to a particular species. Since most passerines such as robins, blue jays, and cardinals utilize open-cup nests, their eggs have protective coloration.

Cardinal nests are often found in urban backyards, although they also nest on forest edges. Their nests are built of twigs, leaves, and grass and normally are located two to five feet above the ground in a tree or bush. One nest I photographed was only two feet from the ground next to the trunk of a small redcedar tree on the edge of a woods. At the turn of the century, cardinals were rare in most of Iowa. Only since the early 1960s have they become common residents over most of the state.

Brown thrashers, like cardinals, are equally at home in backyards or woodlands. They are easy to see when singing, but tend to be sly and secretive near their nests. Caution should be used near a brown thrasher's nest—and all other nests—for disturbance in the area or regular visiting could cause the adult birds to abandon their eggs. Brown thrashers generally prefer nest locations in thick bushes such as gooseberry or multiflora rose, but I once found young birds in a ground nest at the edge of our farm grove.

Planted hedgerows of dogwood, ninebark, honeysuckle, and autumn olive provide summer homesites for brown thrashers, catbirds, cardinals, and a host of other species. Wildlife filmmaker Dick Rassmussen once directed me to the nest of a willow flycatcher in a ninebark shrub on his farm in eastern Marshall County. It was a most unusual nest with a large amount of plant material dangling from the bottom. The willow flycatcher, formerly called Traill's flycatcher, is one of several closely related species often referred to as "empidonax" flycatchers. They are nearly identical in size and markings and almost impossible to identify in the field unless one is familiar with their calls.

Song, vesper, field, savannah, and grasshopper sparrows are among the many birds that nest on or near the ground. Their nests are often subject to predation by garter snakes, bull snakes, skunks, opossums, or raccoons. To counterbalance predation, some ground-nesting species have been known to build five nests in a single season.

The song sparrow conceals its nest in tall grass along streams, near farm buildings, or in fencerows. Field sparrows seem to prefer grassland habitat adjacent to woodland. Vesper, savannah, and grasshopper sparrows are birds of open country. Grasshopper sparrows use short grasses and may tolerate irregular disturbances such as mowing. Savannah sparrows accept moderate disturbance and favor tussocks left by light grazing. Vesper sparrows may even utilize cultivated fields. I once flushed an incubating vesper sparrow from its nest while I was cultivating soybeans. The nest was constructed precisely in the bean row and was unaffected by the cultivator. Some years later I found a vesper sparrow's nest under the leaves of a common dandelion between two corn rows.

Dickcissels, meadowlarks, and bobolinks also prefer grasslands or hayfields as nesting habitat. Most require undisturbed habitat, although bobolinks and meadowlarks frequent grazed pastures. Dickcissels find alfalfa fields to their liking as nesting habitat, although the haymaking process undoubtedly destroys many nests.

The time of year a species chooses to nest is dictated by the availability of food for feeding the young. Great horned owls—Iowa's earliest nesters—begin to lay eggs in late January or early February. As their young are growing up, many small mammals will be available for the growing owlets.

Prairie horned larks are also very early nesters. In late March or early April they line a depression on bare ground with dried grass. Parents incubating eggs can be covered by late spring snows.

Eastern bluebirds drift into Iowa with the gusty winds of early March and are always welcomed as true harbingers of spring. As members of the thrush family, bluebirds prefer semi-open country, especially pastures with large open-grown trees, orchards, or grazed cottonwood-willow creek bottoms. They commonly nest in natural cavities such as old woodpecker holes or hollow broken limbs. The destruction of dead trees and loss of potential nesting cavities caused bluebird numbers to plummet in past years. Trails of birdhouses, maintained by many individuals across the state, have helped bluebirds recover; they have also benefitted black-capped chickadees, tufted titmice, and tree swallows.

Whether birds utilize an open nest, a natural cavity, or a birdhouse, the bulk of Iowa's nesting birds produce young in late spring and early summer. Most feed their young insects and fruits such as raspberries and mulberries. Where mulberries are abundant, they constitute a major source of food for adults and young in June and July. Birds correspondingly spread mulberry seeds (a source of new trees) to fencerows and open fields.

The goldfinch and the yellow-billed cuckoo are two of the last birds to nest each season. The American goldfinch—Iowa's state bird—delays nesting until August, when thistle down is available for lining its nest. It also uses a regurgitated form of thistle seeds to feed its young. The yellow-billed cuckoo prefers to feed its nestlings tent caterpillars, which are most available in late summer. I have seen the young of yellow-billed cuckoos and goldfinches in nests in early September. This may indicate that the first nesting attempt failed, or it may have been a second nesting.

The study of any bird through the nesting season provides insights into its behavior. In central Iowa, migrating red-headed woodpeckers appear during the first week of May. They are striking birds with unmistakable red, white, and black plumage. Their nest cavities are usually high among the dead branches and broken limbs of oaks, maples, or other hardwood trees. After the spread of Dutch elm disease in the 1960s, red-heads often fed and nested in the barren branches and decaying trunks of dead elms. Since these trees lacked leaves, they provided me with better vantage points for observation and photography. The abundance of new nesting sites also may have contributed to a temporary increase in the red-headed woodpecker population.

No other woodpecker is more sought after by birders than the boisterous pileated woodpecker. I searched for this crow-sized bird early in my photographic days. On occasion, I would hear its high-pitched staccato call echo up and down the Iowa River valley in Hardin and Marshall counties. There seemed to be little hope of getting a good photograph of a mature bird until Lyle and Ursula Johnson, from LeGrand, told me about seeing an adult feeding its young at a campsite north of Decorah near Highlandville. One morning in May the three of us set off, and in a matter of hours I stood beneath the nest tree watching and photographing the adults as they fed their nearly fledged young.

The pileated woodpecker has been called the "Great God Woodpecker." In its territory one can often find conspicuous feeding holes in both living and dead trees where it has searched for insects, grubs, and carpenter ants. These holes are sometimes rectangular in shape, or they may appear as long vertical slots cut deep into the trunk of the tree. On numerous occasions I have found these feeding holes close to the base of old trees.

The quest for, and the observation of, nesting birds provides endless opportunities to learn about nature, while bird photography is often spiced with the unexpected. One of my early opportunities at nest photography occurred in 1973 at an indigo bunting nest. Since these buntings prefer edges where brambles and other shrubby vegetation border woods and grassland, farm groves can provide ideal habitat. Although the indigo bunting has always been

Yellow-billed cuckoo brooding young in a small eastern redcedar tree at Prairie Creek Wildlife Refuge, Marshall County.

a common bird where we live, I was not very aware of its presence until I began to recognize the song that the male bird repeatedly sings to proclaim his territory. I simply listened and watched, and eventually I located a nest in tall grass on the edge of our overgrown orchard.

To avoid disturbing them, I observed the birds from a distance throughout the incubation period. When the hatchlings were several days old, I set up my blind about 10 feet from the nest and began to watch the adults bring insects and fruit to the three nestlings. It was in early June, the sunny afternoons were stifling, and the female bunting spent most of her time shading the nest. The cobalt blue male, whose plumage has a metallic sheen, would come to the nest with food and pass it to the female, but he never stayed in the open long enough for a photo.

Four or five days after the eggs hatched, the unexpected occurred. Early one morning, after I had taken up residence in the blind, I noticed that the female was missing. The male bunting was feeding and brooding the young in her absence. At this turn of events, I was able to photograph him as he fed the young.

All seemed to be going well when I heard his frantic distress calls. Peering through my telephoto lens, I saw a small garter snake grasp one of the nestlings and pull the nest from its moorings in the grass. I had invested several weeks in this project and was reluctant to lose the young buntings and potential photographs of the male bird feeding them, so I hurried from the blind, rescued the immature bird from the snake, and replaced the nest in higher grass. The male sensed all was well and went back to food gathering. It was only a temporary solution, however, for the snake was persistent and returned at 45-minute intervals.

Later that morning a female cowbird landed on the open nest and began to peck the young. The male bird was off gathering food and my defense was called for again. With a single parent, added protection was needed if these young were to survive.

Male indigo bunting and young in a grass-supported nest in an old orchard at Prairie Creek Wildlife Refuge, Marshall County.

I summoned my mother, who was in the garden, to watch over the nest. I raced to our shop and quickly constructed a small platform which could be covered with grass to give the young protection from above. A metal rim was installed below the nest to prevent access by snakes. The male bunting immediately accepted the platform, and the young eventually fledged.

Serious observation and intimate knowledge of a bird's habits generally precede successful photography. To locate a nest or perching spot may require days, weeks, months, or years, depending on the particular species. As a result, bird photography usually involves more time and preparation than a beginner can anticipate. To find an active nest of the common yellowthroat one summer, I searched for more than two months.

To photograph red-headed woodpeckers, northern flickers, great horned owls, and a number of other species that nest high in trees, I found it necessary to construct a wooden tower that held an elevated platform upon which I attached a blind. To be eye-level with one red-headed woodpecker nest, the camera and I were 18 feet off the ground. After watching my tower and blind blow over in a strong, gusty wind, I learned that anchors were critical and good insurance.

While most birds adapt quickly to blinds and equipment, photographic activity should not cause undue disturbance to the parent birds and, generally, should not begin until the young are about five days old. There are exceptions, however, for each bird is an individual; some may refuse to accept the presence of a blind near their nest, in which case, one should remove everything from the site.

Since the mid-1980s I have stopped photographing birds at their nests unless I can provide them with predator protection after I have located them. Raccoons investigate most disturbances made by humans; thus photographic activities may indirectly cause predation. As with all wildlife photography, the welfare of the subject should always have first priority.

Cleft phlox on an alluvial sand prairie along the Cedar River, Linn County.

The Prairie Paradox

*T*allgrass prairies that grow on sand exist on the poorest of soil, yet they possess great botanical richness. The mystery behind their magic begins not with sand, but with glacial ice, water, and wind. It is a story revealed by the lay of the land.

During the last 8,000 years most Iowa soils were covered with some form of prairie vegetation. However, prairie floral composition, as with the composition of any other plant community, depends partly on soil type and partly on the climatic effects of latitude, longitude, and slope. Prairie plants, like most others, have evolved to occupy specific niches, and it seems that less-productive soils generally have the greatest species diversity.

Sandy soils were ground in glacial mills; their origin stretches back to the ice itself. The melting of the Des Moines Lobe, an appendage of the widespread Wisconsin ice sheet, proceeded gradually from central Iowa, as seasonal temperatures permitted, until it left northern Iowa about 12,500 years ago. In its wake remained an unsorted mixture of clay, sand, gravel, and boulders called glacial till. This provided the parent material for most of north central Iowa's productive topsoil, although the manner in which the soil was derived varies considerably. The effects of glacial till deposits are apparent not only where we live on the terminal moraine of this last glacial contact in central Iowa but also a few miles to the east of us where glacial ice mantled the land 600,000 years ago when pre-Illinoian ice sheets covered the Midwest.

As the Wisconsin ice gradually disappeared from the upper Midwest, meltwater carved new valleys and flooded and enlarged old ones that lay beyond the glacier's reach. During summer seasons, excessively high water volumes carried silts and sands in suspension and deposited these alluvial particles on broad valley bottomlands. During low-flow winter seasons, sparse protective vegetation on the valley floors allowed strong northwest winds to pick up the exposed silts and sands and redeposit them, sometimes many miles away. No prehistoric records describe these events for us, but it's probably safe to assume that dust storms of the 1930s were little more than afternoon dust devils when compared to such annual silt blizzards.

These windblown deposits of loess were thickest near their origin, and their depth rapidly diminished as distance from the source increased. Since the wind sorts material as it is transported, the smallest particles are naturally carried the greatest distance. Loess, which is German for "loose" and is generally pronounced "luss," formed 40 percent of Iowa's best cropland. Edwin Way Teale called it the "Golden Earth of Agriculture" because of its importance as a soil parent material. Rarely on earth, however, are its features more prominent than along the east side of the Missouri River valley in western Iowa and northern Missouri, where loess deposits ranging from 60 to 200 feet thick form steep bluffs at the edge of the floodplain. Unlike the topsoil on our farm in central Iowa, which is littered with ice-deposited glacial debris, loess is stone-free.

Sand deposited along most major rivers and streams during periods of high water flow may form a streamside alluvial terrace. Botanically these areas are quite similar to upland sand prairies but may be surrounded by bottomland forest. Due to their location at or near the floodplain, they may be subject to disturbance when flooding occurs. Cedar Bend Savanna along the Cedar River north of Cedar Falls in Black Hawk County is one such sand prairie. Black oak and bur oak dominate, while typical prairie savanna species colonize openings. Along the Cedar River north of Cedar Rapids, cleft phlox occurs on sand deposits in open oak woodland. A demure plant, its pale blue flowers scarcely show among the fallen leaves and mosses of early spring.

The largest contiguous alluvial sand prairie in Iowa is the Big Sand Mound, a 420-acre nature preserve along the Mississippi River south of Muscatine that is owned and managed by the MidAmerican Energy Company. Shifting sand dunes have long been a part of the Big Sand Mound, and vegetation constantly tries to stabilize its loose friable structure. In early June, we see goat's rue, along with erect dayflower, dwarf dandelion, and grasses such as three-awn and June grass, covering large open areas. Minute plants such as British-soldier and reindeer lichen grow on bare sand beneath sparse grass.

We have visited this xeric (dry) site a number of times, and the plants always show a response to the season's weather. After the wet summer of 1993, the vegetation was lush, with heavy stands of big bluestem and colorful forbs such as Missouri goldenrod and rough blazing-stars. Some of the blazing-star stalks had nearly 150 rosettes. It had been a very good year; these plants were not wanting for moisture.

The Big Sand Mound provides critical habitat for a number of amphibians and reptiles, including the six-lined racerunner, a whiptail lizard, and the Eastern hognose snake, which is known for its ability to turn upside down and play dead. The two best-known species—the endangered Illinois mud turtle, a subspecies of the yellow mud turtle; and the ornate box turtle—both use the sand dunes as breeding grounds.

After the original loess deposition, periodic episodes of

favorable conditions enabled the wind to move alluvial sand from lowlands and redeposit it upon adjoining uplands, again to the southeast or leeward of its source. Iowa's windblown, or eolian, sand deposits are small and widely scattered and often are long and narrow. Although they are scarcely a drop-in-the-bucket when compared to the Nebraska Sand Hills, they comprise a significant soil type southeast of most major drainage basins.

I have spent most of my time on upland sand prairies that exist on eolian sand. The history of one small area near our home begins to unfold when I look out our east kitchen window. The nearest old trees are just-visible silhouettes on the skyline where the sun dawns in early November and late February. On this distant hilltop, a few old bur oaks remain of a prairie savanna. An adjacent north-facing hillside is still covered with red oaks, white oaks, and the occasional basswood. This woodland marks the western end of a thin gallery forest along meandering Minerva Creek in western Marshall County. Splinter forests, as such, were never more than remnants, with gains and losses in size directly proportional to the frequency of prairie fires, which, until pioneer settlement, always carried the upper hand here in Iowa's heartland.

Minerva Creek, a tributary of the Iowa River, flows to the east and south just north of our farm, with a short branch dissecting our quarter section from southwest to northeast. It is a fairly young stream in geologic terms and may have carried away some of the first meltwater from the leading edge of the Des Moines Lobe, for it was only about 14,000 years ago that the massive ice sheet ground to a halt and started melting precisely where our farmstead stands today.

As we follow Minerva Creek toward the Iowa River, it is an open textbook of geologic happenings. Soil types change dramatically from pebbly glacial till, dropped by the melting ice, to fine-textured windblown loess and sand-mantled ridges. In less than 30 miles, three major parent materials of Iowa's soils are found. On

Rough blazing-stars and Missouri goldenrod on the Big Sand Mound, Muscatine County.

one sandy upland, the 17-acre Marietta Sand Prairie survives.

Like most Iowans, I knew little about sand prairies until I was formally introduced. One hot, humid, windy July afternoon Dr. Roger Landers took me to the Mark Sand Prairie, a privately owned tract in Black Hawk County. Only 36 acres in the midst of intensive Iowa agriculture, this prairie relict went undiscovered by botanists until 1969. Shortly thereafter, Glenn Crum, an Iowa State University graduate student, studied it intensively and prepared a species list. Once the site's uniqueness was apparent, its protection became a prime goal for the Iowa Chapter of The Nature Conservancy. Some years later, the area was acquired and renamed the Cedar Hills Sand Prairie. Since the initial purchase, it has been expanded to 90 acres. It wasn't the first time an important natural area had gone unnoticed in Iowa's maze of grainfields, nor will it be the last. Since 1969, numerous small prairie tracts and some that are more than 100 acres in size have been discovered across the state.

Sand prairies often possess the typical swells, swales, and marshes characteristic of rich loam prairies, yet their flora may be very different. Swales are often filled with ferns, sedges, and sphagnum moss that form hummocks and make walking difficult. Uplands that are only slightly higher but are much drier may have sparse grass but great concentrations of colorful forbs.

Soil structure provides the key to the many obvious differences between sand and loam prairies. Eolian sand is flyspeck in size, up to one millimeter in diameter, and flows through one's fingers like crystals through an hourglass. Loam crumbles on contact, for its structure is based on humus, which holds together its mixture of sand, silt, and clay particles. Fractures occur along irregular lines and form tiny lumps called peds. Rarely is enough humus present in sand to make peds.

Practically no runoff occurs on sandy soil regardless of rainfall amount, but little moisture is retained because of its porous texture and low humus content. This excessive water permeability

*Sensitive ferns and meadowsweet in a sand prairie bog at the Marietta
Sand Prairie State Preserve, Marshall County.*

causes leaching of nutrients, especially calcium, to lower soil horizons and severely limits productive plant growth. Moisture gradients can be traced easily in the vegetation types as one moves from the driest uplands, where only the deepest-rooted species thrive, toward the wetter swales and marshes. On loam prairies this moisture limitation would be apparent only on the driest ridges.

On sand prairies, however, a mesic, or moist, prairie band between wet swale and dry prairie contains not only lush growth but also frequently has the greatest variety of species. Where swales or standing water occur, the depth of sand over less-permeable materials such as glacial till may be shallow. Thus the water table may surface and form marshes, shallow lakes, or very wet swales. Loam swales often have closed centers, but it is a rare year when the moisture level remains constant throughout the summer season. Sand prairie swales, on the other hand, are often bog-like in nature, which may account for the profusion of marsh ferns, sensitive ferns, and, in some cases, quaking aspens.

The floral composition of any prairie relict depends not only on soil drainage but also on its size, the number of years it has escaped overgrazing, and the extent of "weed spraying" activities by landowners, their neighbors, or the county highway department. It is a rare tract that we have not tried to drain, plow, or overgraze if it contains standing room for at least one cow. Thus natural inhabitants of most old pastures, odd corners of cropland, and wet prairies have been fighting battles for survival since settlement.

Oddly enough, sand prairies seem to have been less affected by landowners for several reasons. Perforated pipe (tile) is often laid underground to facilitate drainage. However, sand plugs tile, so wet areas are quite difficult to drain. Introduced pasture species, such as brome grass, may not survive because of moisture and nutrient limitations which favor better-adapted natives. For the same reasons, grain crops may yield poorly except in "ideal" years, making sandy soil farming a risky crop investment without irrigation.

Of Iowa's remaining prairie relicts, sand prairies are the most unusual; each contains a unique assemblage of plants. A close look at individual sites reveals both striking similarities and inconsistencies. Of the three sand prairies I am most familiar with, the swale of one contains quaking aspens; the other two do not. Two have large stands of rough blazing-stars; one has none. All three lack compass-plants, which grow on loam prairies within a few miles of each. It is said that cattle have a sweet tooth for the huge oak-like leaves, so perhaps a past history of moderate grazing on all three areas has accounted for the demise of compass-plants. A lush stand of sand lovegrass predominates in the upland of the Marietta Sand Prairie near my home; it is absent from the other sites. All areas lack the severe invasion by alien plants which tend to predominate on continuously grazed loam prairies. Of the 280 species that were found on the 36-acre Cedar Hills Sand Prairie, only 22 were not native. The majority of these grew near boundary fences where cattle disturbances had been the greatest. Since the cattle have been removed, non-native species appear to be decreasing.

In April the growing season's kaleidoscope of color begins deep in the hummocky swale, where marsh marigolds glow mellow gold. A few weeks later on dry uplands, sky-blue faces of giant bird's-foot violets rise among dried auburn clumps of winter-weathered little bluestem. By June, a soft yellow haze of hairy puccoon spreads across the driest zones, which may be no more than 50 steps away from, or 10 feet above, a nearby swale.

Sand prairies, like most prairies, have only hints of color in early spring, unlike the rich woods where spring flowers near their grand finale by late May. Early in June, clumps of blue flag iris and the pink spikes of wild sweet-william appear in the swales and along the edges of greening marshes. An occasional shooting-star may also make its debut, but great concentrations of these meteors-come-to-earth are generally restricted to the heavier soils of loam prairies. July's black-eyed Susans, Culver's root, hoary vervain, and tall meadow rue prepare the way for the wild extravaganza of blazing-stars.

Both the rough and tall blazing-stars generally thrive on these nutrient-starved soils. They are among the deepest rooted of all prairie plants; their root systems may extend to 15 feet below the soil surface. The magenta torches of tall blazing-stars, which grow near the swales, light the way in late July and early August. Often they are mixed with that strange member of the carrot family known as rattlesnake-masters, an umbelliferae with yucca-like leaves. A few weeks later, tall stalks of rough blazing-stars, with up to 60 rosettes on each stalk, color the driest land with various shades of reddish purple, depending upon the lighting. Over a period of about two weeks, flowers gradually descend each stalk until the last light is blown out in mid-September.

During the color peak in late August 1974, I spent nearly five hours with my parents wandering, awestruck, among 15 acres of rough blazing-stars on the Cedar Hills Sand Prairie. Adequate rainfall and a spring burn had triggered the optimum display from every plant. The scene was quite simply beyond description. We saw a similar display on the Kisk-Ke-Kosh Sand Prairie in Jasper County in 1976, but I have not seen or heard of a comparable display in the intervening years on either area.

Beneath the canopy of color, which, like a view of mountains, tends to distort one's vision, less-conspicuous grasses have carried on their undercover movement since early May. Cool-season species, such as porcupine grass, June grass, and bluejoint in the swales, are the first to appear and remain only as dead stalks by midsummer. Most of the grasses are warm-season species and do not put forth flowers or seeds until late August or early September. On the driest sand, hairy grama, side-oats grama, little bluestem, paspalum, and sand lovegrass each flourish as space and moisture conditions permit. In the mesic zone of the prairie, lush stands of switchgrass, big bluestem, and Indian grass provide the tall compo-

Rough blazing-stars, Missouri goldenrod, and paspalum in the Cedar Hills Sand Prairie State Preserve, Blackhawk County.

nent on an otherwise shortgrass prairie upland. Deep in the swales, rice cut-grass, dwarfed by the tall flowering heads of slough grass, is accompanied by water hemlock, Joe Pye-weed, the woody spiraea called meadowsweet, and fragrant clusters of swamp milkweed, an insect favorite. Half a dozen species of goldenrod mingle with the blazing-stars and introduce September asters and bottle gentians. Some species may continue to flower into October, bringing up "parade's end" well after the first autumn frost.

Sand prairies aren't common in tallgrass country, although new areas will likely be discovered along the streams and rivers of eastern Iowa. Most people have never heard of them, let alone walked upon one. They comprise only a few hundred of Iowa's 35 million acres. They offer some of the best wildlife habitat for grassland birds such as sedge wrens, bobolinks, and grasshopper, vesper, and field sparrows. The mere existence of sand prairies is a seeming paradox: for all their richness, they have survived because of poor soil. Their continued existence is a testimonial to natural adaptation at its best.

Wild roses, sand lovegrass, and white sage in autumn color at the
Marietta Sand Prairie State Preserve, Marshall County.

Skunk cabbage flower and new leaves at Hanging Bog, Linn County.

Woodland Wildflowers

Spring advances in spite of winter's icy crust. Its first stirrings occur in swampy woodlands with the emergence of skunk cabbage, Iowa's earliest wildflower. Coldness prevails, yet its great spearheads poking through the muck assure us that a season of life-giving warmth will once again return. Skunk cabbage is only one of several hundred plants that can be found in Iowa woodlands.

I always eagerly await the emergence of these denizens of Iowa's forest. Wildflowers are the hope and promise of spring—nature's renewal and resurrection. If the works of Rembrandt were to be hung at a local gallery, few of us would miss the showing. Yet an equally grand display of nature's form, color, and fragrance occurs annually in the spring woods. We miss the eternal essence of spring when we fail to take a forest walk. No two spring seasons in a given woodland are the same; each is part of a very broad and complex picture. The timing of the warm-up, and whether spring rains occur early or late in the season, dramatically alter what is visible from one year to the next.

Throughout Iowa, forest communities exhibit many similarities, yet no two woodlands are exactly the same. A north-facing slope is always cooler than a south-facing slope across the valley.

Temperature differences, as well as the amount of sunlight, affect the species composition of the nonwoody or herbaceous understory, which includes most wildflowers.

Skunk cabbage, for example, has specific site requirements. It can be found in several northeast Iowa counties and in Muscatine County in the southeast. However, Hanging Bog in Linn County probably protects the state's largest patch. It may also be the most southwestern U.S. location for this plant's natural distribution, which stretches to the eastern seaboard, north to southern Canada, and south to the Carolinas.

Hanging Bog, a rich upland forest dominated by red oak and basswood, lies just southwest of the Cedar River floodplain between Palo and Cedar Rapids. The small bog appears much like a sidehill seep. It was created by a hard water spring that produced a series of lime deposits that have slumped, forming terraces along a north-facing slope. Because the terraces are water-logged throughout the year, the bog-like effect is produced.

Flowers of skunk cabbage begin to grow as early as mid-February, when the ground is frozen. A metabolic change within the plant produces heat, which melts the snow and thaws the soil around it. Shortly after the mottled greenish-maroon hood—the flower's spathe—is above ground, it begins to unfold, revealing a dome-like spadix. The spadix is covered with small yellow flowers; each flower has one pistil, four stamens, and four sepals. Often the spadix is nearly obscured by tiny anthers loaded with yellow pollen.

Few insects abound in mid-March because of cold temperatures, yet the flowers are insect-pollinated. Early honeybees, gnats, carrion flies, and snowflies are attracted to the flower's foul skunk-like odor. Botanist Roger Knudson of Luther College in Decorah, who has studied the plant extensively, found that a small spider is usually associated with the flower, although its role in pollination is uncertain. Late in March, a week or two after the first flowers appear, tightly rolled cones of leaves begin to emerge next to the plant.

If we return to Hanging Bog in mid-June, we discover the skunk cabbage has continued to grow and dominate the woodland bog. Plants which were mere spears in March's frozen earth are now three feet in height and have huge cabbage-like leaves called elephant ears. In early summer, red berries attached near the base of the plant indicate maturing fruits. As summer advances, the berries lose their scarlet color, turn brown, and grow about as large as a small acorn. By late summer, the large leaves have wilted down and the seeds have begun to fall from the pods. They are not an important wildlife food, but some seeds will be eaten by ruffed grouse, pheasants, bobwhite quail, and wood ducks. Browsing animals such as deer and cattle may disturb the tall plants by trampling but generally avoid eating them because of their strong odor and stinging acrid taste.

Skunk cabbage has a huge taproot surrounded by lateral roots which not only anchor the plant but also continually pull it into the ground as it grows. Thus transplanting an adult plant is nearly impossible. However, seeds grow easily if they are simply placed on soft mucky soil with consistent moisture. Like many wild plants, they grow slowly, take several years to begin producing seeds, and may live to a very old age—perhaps 100 years or more.

Many writers of books on wild foods attest to the palatability of skunk cabbage as a cooked vegetable, but probably few have sampled their own recipes. In his book *Stalking the Healthful Herbs*, the late Euell Gibbons related his experiment of cooking up a batch of fresh skunk cabbage leaves. The first thing to go wrong was the smell, since other authorities on wild foods unanimously agreed that "no trace of odor was given off while cooking." Gibbons quickly found out the other authors were right, for the thick foul stench which permeated his kitchen could hardly be described as a "trace." A visit by an angry skunk would have left it no worse. Upon sampling it, he found it tasted just like it smelled. In addition to the smell and the taste, swallowing a small portion left a burning sensation in his throat, just as would a bite of Jack-in-the-pulpit. Both plants contain calcium oxalate crystals, which penetrate mucus membranes of the mouth and throat and cause swelling and severe pain.

With further experimentation, Gibbons discovered that excellent-tasting skunk cabbage pancakes could be made by drying either the leaves or roots for six months, then grinding them into a flour, and mixing it half and half with wheat flour to make the batter. Dry, crisp, easily crumpled leaves also made an old-fashioned herb-meat cabbage pudding which he described as "eminently edible." He had, at last, conquered the smell, taste, and fire of skunk cabbage. Thorough drying seems to be the secret of success.

The leaves of Indian poke, found in the eastern United States, are very poisonous and resemble those of skunk cabbage. Thorough identification is a must if you are planning to use skunk cabbage for food.

At Hanging Bog and in native forests throughout the state, one can usually find a wide variety of woodland wildflowers. Sharp-lobed hepatica and snow trillium open in late March or during early April. In southern Iowa they may flower two or more weeks before those in northern counties. I have even seen plants in full flower growing in cracks on north-facing sandstone cliffs in central Iowa during May.

Hepatica, which is sometimes called liverleaf, is normally restricted to north-facing slopes. Its flower color varies from white to pink but can also be deep blue; new leaves emerge just as the petals begin to fade. As in many other species, the flower's opening is light-activated, a phototropic movement or response. If you go for a walk when it is cloudy or in the late evening, hepatica may have closed up shop for the day and can be quite difficult to recognize among the fallen leaves on the forest floor.

Snow trilliums, on the other hand, open and stay open day and night, warm days or cold. I have seen their flower petals and leaves frost-covered. They are well adapted in the woodland com-

Sharp-lobed hepatica in mixed sugar maple–red oak deciduous forest at Hardin City State Preserve, Hardin County.

munity and spread abundantly where competition from other woodland species has been reduced. In an overgrazed woods I have seen snow trilliums appear, as their name implies, like snow on the ground, although this is not the normal situation in undisturbed woods.

Bloodroots usually follow snow trilliums and hepaticas. Sap which exudes from a broken bloodroot stem is red and easily stains one's fingers. The pure white flowers are generally short-lived. In less than a week, the newly emerged rounded leaves are surrounded by white flower petals scattered on the ground. Bloodroot is currently being studied by medical researchers, since it contains compounds which have the potential to prevent tooth decay.

Dutchman's breeches usually flowers when bloodroots are dropping their petals. The real challenge with this species is to find its look-alike cousin, squirrel corn. The two may grow side by side on wooded hillsides. I have as much difficulty locating squirrel corn as finding spring morels.

Green shoots and leaves begin to appear throughout most woodlands by mid-April. Some spring ephemerals, such as rue anemone, flower immediately; others, such as Virginia bluebells, grow vegetatively until late April or early May. Rue anemone often flowers on warm south-facing hillsides by mid-April but holds off until early May on north-facing slopes. False rue anemone flowers are long-lasting and can form white blankets on the mucky soil of some forest floodplains by the end of the first week of May.

In the same type of habitat one can find Virginia bluebells carpeting bottomlands along many rivers and streams. They, too, seem to prefer soggy soils beneath old silver maples, American elms, boxelders, and cottonwoods. One dramatic display of Virginia bluebells we never miss covers most of the rich floodplain soil along Honey Creek at Reece's County Park in southern Hardin County. Under overcast lighting, they blue the entire understory.

Downy yellow violets prefer the shade of open woods, while the common blue violet thrives where there is more sunlight on the edge of woods and in forest openings. Jack-in-the pulpit is a favorite which blossoms in mid- to late May in most rich woods. Its unique flower is bilaterally symmetrical. In shaded ravines, the plants can be nearly two feet high. Leek, or wild garlic, has linear leaves with parallel veins and a very pleasant smell, providing you like garlic. The whitish flower is rarely seen, as it blooms in summer after the leaves have withered. As an herb, it was often used by pioneers and Native Americans for seasoning.

Mayapples poke up through fallen leaves with Solomon's seals in April, but the flowers do not appear until mid-May and only occur on plants with two leaves. They are just one of a host of species which flower in the warming spring woods. Woodland phlox, or "sweet-william," often blossoms with mayapples. Its flower cluster is lavender blue. The plants, which easily self-seed, spread into open meadows and roadside ditches seeking sunlight. Merrybells, or bellwort, has a dangling yellow flower with a slight twist. The leaves are similar to those of Solomon's seal, but the stem of merrybells penetrates the base of each leaf, thus it is sometimes called perfoliate bellwort.

In mid- to late May, one can look for seedpods on bloodroots. They are covered by the leaves and split open in a matter of days. If one's timing is right, the seeds can be gathered and scattered in the leaf litter to start new patches of bloodroots. As the leaves of bluebells begin to turn yellow and dry up, their seeds can be harvested and planted in a similar manner.

In late May or early June, when the red-eyed vireo begins singing his territorial song, it is time to look for flowers of the three species of Solomon's seals. True Solomon's seal, false Solomon's seal, and starry false Solomon's seal prevail in Iowa woodlands. All are members of the lily family and start out as a green spear poking up through the leaf litter. When they bloom, the flower shape and location of blossoms on the plant make it easy to distinguish one species from another.

Wild geranium, wild columbine, Virginia waterleaf, and sweet cicely flower toward the end of May, when the chance of finding mosquitoes and no-see-ums in the woods has dramatically improved. Virginia waterleaf and sweet cicely, among the most common woodland plants, may overwhelm the leaves and flowers of most other species. Wild columbine and miterwort often grow on sandstone or limestone outcrops along with fragile ferns, the common polypody fern, maidenhair ferns, and bulblet bladder ferns.

Boreal forest plants, left behind when coniferous forests retreated northward following the melting glaciers, continue to persist in places like White Pine Hollow and Bixby State Preserves. Twinleaf can be found in shaded ravines in parts of northeast Iowa from Bremer County to Dubuque County. Beneath dense white pine stands where thick mats of needles form the turf, one may encounter rattlesnake plantain. It has a whorl of bicolored leaves with a strange, almost checkerboard pattern. Though the plant lacks showy flowers, its leaves are evergreen and can be seen in midwinter on snow-free slopes.

Showy orchis seems to respond to light from the open canopy of aspen stands; it is one of our orchids that still thrives in good numbers. Nodding trilliums can be found, often on north-facing slopes, in many rich woods. Where conditions are ideal, they occasionally grow in great abundance. Prairie trilliums can be found in southeast Iowa north to Linn County; their dark red sepals accent mottled leaves.

Iowa golden saxifrage, bunchberry, twinflower, monkshood, lyre-leafed rock cress, and kidney-leaved violet are plants of algific slopes. Unlike most north-facing slopes, cold air flowing from underlying rock strata cools these steep hillsides during the summer months. To a botanist, it is a microclimate where plants with very specific habitat requirements survive. In the case of algific slopes, the plants are more characteristic of northern forests.

Along the Mississippi River, on ridgetops and slopes where

Miterwort, woodland phlox, maidenhair fern, and true Solomon's seal at Doliver State Park, Webster County.

exposed limestone or sandstone occurs, one can find the jeweled shooting-star blooming in mid-May. Its flower varies from a delicate pink to deep magenta and has the fragrance of very fine perfume. The rosette of leaves resembles an immature dandelion; occasionally it occurs in mowed lawns along the Mississippi River bluffs. I once found several dozen plants growing around the base of an old white oak on the blufftop at Turkey River Mounds State Preserve. Although it was nearly 20 years ago, the scene is still fresh in my mind.

From midsummer through early autumn a few species make dramatic showings. In July the tall bellflower can be found on woodland edges and clearings. During August, false dragonhead, jewelweed, and cardinal flower provide nectar for migrating hummingbirds; all three plants seem to prefer the wet soils of bottomlands and marsh edges. False dragonhead (also called obedient plant) has often been used as an attractive addition in perennial gardens. Juice from a crushed stem of jewelweed relieves the itch from contact with stinging nettle and poison ivy. I have most frequently encountered the cardinal flower on floodplains of the Mississippi River.

In August, one may find white snakeroot throughout the woods and thin-leaved coneflower on woodland edges. These plants readily self-seed and can easily take over a small rock garden.

Late in summer, before the sumac turns scarlet, we can find the woodland sunflower and green-headed coneflower. A variety of woodland asters bloom throughout the autumn color season and after the first frosts. Smooth aster, heart-leaved aster, and azure aster can all be found on woodland edges and in clearings.

No wildland can ever be experienced in its entirety on a single trip or two, or even a hundred. Natural communities are dynamic—that is, constantly changing and being renewed—yet their natural order is timeless. As we search for wildflowers in Iowa woodlands, we find new opportunities season after season, year after year.

Prairie trilliums and creeping fragile ferns in mixed deciduous forest in Jefferson County.

Jeweled shooting-stars around the base of an old white oak at Turkey River Mounds State Preserve, Clayton County.

Light from the sunrise streaming in from behind the island through rising steam on Lower Pine Lake, Pine Lake State Park, Hardin County.

The Magic Light

L ight is the prime ingredient of our visual process, and under certain weather conditions, it can transform our view of an ordinary landscape, plant, or animal. It is not a frequent event, but when it happens we too are transformed. It is like a vision which opens our eyes.

Weather conditions and time of day affect the perceived color of vegetation and the land. Before sunrise on a clear morning, light reflected from the sky has some of the same qualities as an overcast day; however, it contains large amounts of blue and can make green vegetation appear cyan. Just after sunrise, direct light from the sun has the opposite effect; it is warm and contains large amounts of red because the slanting rays must pass through more atmosphere, which absorbs more blue light than it does when the sun is overhead. Thus the world we see before and after sunrise, and at sunset, is far different than that of midday. On a number of occasions I have captured the effects of both kinds of light in a single image. In the earth's beginning, there was the struggle between fire and ice. We can still see it in the light of dawn and dusk.

Photography is always the search for perfect light. Rainy, cloudy days are much better than bright, sunny ones for the observation of wildlife and natural communities. Because the light is diffused and of low contrast, we can see through the woods and into thick vegetation. Just as we can see more under an overcast sky, the camera records better in low-contrast light. It is often best just before and after storms. On occasion I have spent entire days working in light rain and mist. Under these conditions, wildflowers and green leaves are rich and vibrant and wildlife may be more active.

The dramatic contrast of "Ross" light often occurs before and after rainstorms. This concept came to me after reading the canoeing adventures of nature writer Sigurd Olson, who wrote of his encounter with Frank Ross of the *Saturday Evening Post*: "I discovered with him that unusual effects could be achieved during certain rare moments when the light was just right, that color and depth were accentuated to the point where ordinary scenes could become spectacular pictures." From Olson's description I understood Ross lighting to be that moment when the sun breaks through a heavy overcast sky. When it happens just after sunrise or just before sunset, great contrast between the sunlit foreground and the dark sky transforms the entire scene. This phenomenon occurs rarely, but when it does, there are great photographic opportunities. Olson wrote further: "No two ever see it alike, but this much is true, somewhere within it is a power that transfigures everything, even those who watch."

Northern lights are visible in Iowa about 10 times a year. The aurora borealis, as it is more properly called, is fluorescent in nature; it takes place in the ionosphere, 60 to 80 miles above the earth, when high-energy electrons from the sun encounter atmospheric oxygen and nitrogen. These electrons are trapped in the earth's magnetic field and diverted toward the poles. At our latitude, northern lights often appear as little more than a faint greenish glow just above the northern horizon. On rare occasions the curtains of light, which seem to move and range from green to red, extend from just above the horizon to directly overhead.

Spring green of black walnut trees in an afternoon thunderstorm at Prairie Creek Wildlife Refuge, Marshall County.

I have seen the best displays in fall and winter. One winter morning about 5:00 A.M. I photographed the curtains of colored light with stars in the background. It was a cold, damp early morning hour and it would have been easy to watch through a window in our warm house and then go back to bed, but nature's best moments do not always occur when it is comfortable or convenient. We must not fail to take advantage of them—the opportunity may not occur again.

Like few other weather events, winter ice storms can transform an entire landscape. I recorded the results of one ice storm; in the early light, the scene was dazzling. Ice-encased branches, buds, and wires were transformed from crystal formations to glowing embers while soft snow turned burnt amber.

By midday the landscape had turned to pure silver. Trees stood like giant chandeliers veiled with diamonds. Creeks became palace corridors with blue water floors and sparkling walls. Everywhere I looked the landscape had been touched by a magic wand and transformed into a fairyland. The wind subsided as sundown approached, and the mellow light changed the ice from silver to gold. Fences surrounding each field glittered like jewel-shrouded necklaces. Grasses burned like tiny torches over the snow-covered ground. As the sun set, the lights flickered out and a full moon began to rise in the eastern sky. In the moonlight, the ice-covered branches twinkled like tinsel against the starlit heavens. It was a dreamworld that continued throughout the night.

Seasonal weather change may be difficult to detect. Day-length shortens with each passing day after the summer solstice and the sun's warming rays become less direct. Cooling nighttime temperatures gradually gain ground to give us the first hint of autumn in late August. On cool, clear nights radiation fog forms in valleys, creeping in with the stealth of a nighttime invader. Over lakes and creeks, steam rises in gentle wisps like smoke from a snuffed candle. In early morning light, the sun's first rays give mist

Northern lights about 5:00 A.M. at Prairie Creek Wildlife Refuge, Marshall County.

Meadowfly covered with frozen dew in early morning light at Prairie Creek Wildlife Refuge, Marshall County.

an ethereal quality unlike fog in midday.

Light frost may accompany lowland fog even as early as late August. One morning in the halflight of dawn I came upon an unbelievable sight. Along our prairie creek a meadowfly clinging to a dried grass stalk was lightly glazed with frozen dew. Its gossamer wings glowed like a jeweled brooch against a dark backdrop of old cottonwoods and willows. It remained in a state of torpor until heat from the sun's first rays transformed the ice into golden dew and finally dried its wings to bring freedom and flight. There was magic in the morning light.

Algific (cold air) slope in a cold spring rain at Bluebell Hollow, Clayton County.

The Photographic Record

M y first photographs were taken while I was a sophomore in high school on a Future Farmers of America trip to Colorado in the summer of 1961. I used my father's old Kodak Number Two Folding Autographic Brownie. It took 2¼" x 3¼" negatives on 120 film. When I inherited the camera, it was nearly 50 years old and had a light leak in the bellows. When I look back at the photos I took on that trip—now more than 30 years ago—the photographs are quite similar in style to those I take today. My favorite views were of natural scenes such as rock slides, mountains, and rushing streams.

I continued to use the camera and eventually took photos with it on another trip west to Montana and Colorado in 1963. The light leaks were worse on this trip, although I had attempted to use electrical tape to fix the corners of the bellows. They caused some damage to most of the images, but I still managed to get some very acceptable views.

In the fall of 1967 I convinced my parents to let me buy an Asahi Pentax single lens reflex camera in the 35-mm format and a 300-mm Soligor telephoto lens. Gaige Wunder, a friend at Iowa State University, helped me order it from Lee's and Lo's Camera

Company in Hong Kong, since their prices were 30 percent below retail for a comparable Honeywell Pentax. Due to trademark restrictions on imported cameras, customs officials usually required that the brand name be scratched from the front of the camera. For some unknown reason my camera made it through customs unmarked. This of course seemed to be the answer to my dreams.

My first roll of film, a roll of Kodachrome X, proved to be a disaster. After loading the film, I was uncertain it was hooked up properly and rewound it into the canister by mistake. To retrieve the film leader, I pried the canister open and, in the process, exposed the entire roll. Needless to say, it did not bolster my confidence in either the camera or my photographic ability. My next 10 or so rolls were taken on Anscochrome 500. It was a high-speed film for that time which enabled me to hand-hold the camera on almost every occasion. I certainly didn't want to be bothered with a tripod, so it was my film of choice for the first six or so months.

It was not long, however, until I began to see that this high-speed film was quite grainy and short on color saturation. I then went back to Kodachrome and began shooting what was known at that time as Kodachrome II (#2), a 25 ISO film which was slow but had a nearly nonexistent grain structure and great color saturation. I continued to use this film and its later version, Kodachrome 25, as well as Kodachrome 64 until I was married in 1988. Then my wife and I decided it was just too confusing to use two different types of 35-mm film and we settled on Kodachrome 64.

I graduated from Iowa State University in the spring of 1968 and by midsummer was drafted into the U.S. Army and sent to Fort Bliss in the Texas desert for boot camp. After the eight-week training period I was assigned to Rocky Mountain Arsenal, just outside of Denver, Colorado. To many of my associates this was an army vacation post in the middle of the Vietnam War. I immediately flew home to retrieve my car so I would have transportation to see the Colorado mountains. A week or so later I took my first trip to

Loveland Pass. It was cold, but I obtained a few photographs of sunlit peaks and Steller's jays. Although our base of operations was Denver, we had two other sites in California where I was to be sent after orientation. Shortly after Christmas in 1969 temporary duty orders came down for me to go to Edwards Air Force Base in the Mojave Desert in south central California. This post is famous for its dry lake beds, which serve as runways for test aircraft and, more recently, as a landing site for the Space Shuttle. Our site of operations was not on the base proper but near its periphery in relatively undisturbed desert.

I quickly became enamored with the desert despite its often hostile weather. One day would be warm and windless; the next, bitterly cold with a 40- to 50-mile-per-hour wind blowing sand and dirt. Serious dust storms were common occurrences, since abandoned farm fields had little or no protective vegetation. The blowing dust sandblasted automotive paint and windshields. Our post had a number of open fields, but around us were Joshua trees and creosote bushes. With plenty of wildland nearby, I began to explore whenever there was an opportunity and soon learned some of the desert's unique vegetation. Although it was an unusually dry year, I saw many desert flowers for the first time that spring.

Mandatory transfers occurred every six months when a person was on temporary duty; thus in late fall I was sent to Beale Air Force Base near the towns of Marysville and Yuba City in the upper Sacramento valley. I began to think seriously about a larger format camera and soon found an old 4" x 5" format Speed Graphic. It came with a standard 127-mm Ektar lens. I was not really sure what I needed at the time or if I would know how to use the camera, but I decided to buy it and take a chance. It was on sale for $150, about a month's base pay at the time. One Saturday I took the camera and my first sheets of 4" x 5" Ektachrome and headed for Lake Tahoe, about 100 miles away. Enroute I found some nicely sunlit waterfalls in the high Sierras and made a number of exposures of Lake Tahoe

*Edward's hairstreak on butterfly milkweed in a prairie remnant at
Talmage Hill, Union County.*

from its west shoreline. These were my first successful 4" x 5" images, and even today I consider them quite publishable. Much of the winter in this part of California is overcast with rain. I remember one particularly dreary three-week spell without sunshine when it rained at least part of every day. I longed to return to the desert sunshine of the Mojave.

Late in the winter of 1969 I was reassigned to Edwards just in time for spring flowers. After my first outings I became aware that I could not make the lens tip or swing as a view camera should to obtain great depth of field. This photographic technique, based on the Scheimpflug principle, aligns the plane of focus with the film plane and was of prime importance to my style of photography. I studied the situation and finally decided on a solution. I took the front lens support into our machine shop and modified it with a bench grinder so the lens would tip and swing in any position yet could be locked tight when it came time to take the picture. I performed the operation with great reluctance, for there was the possibility I would ruin the camera. The change in design worked, however, just as I had hoped. It was now possible to get great depth of field in any scene simply by tipping the lens forward. During that spring I also purchased a new 210-mm Schneider Symmar lens which I deemed necessary for close-ups. I was excited about trying both the lens and the camera.

Winter rains had been respectable in late 1969 and in early 1970. By the first week in April the sand was yellow with desert dandelions and coreopsis. In the foothills west of Lancaster, California poppies glowed a golden orange which could be seen from a distance of several miles in the clear desert air. The area is now protected as a California poppy preserve.

Early one Saturday morning I drove into the foothills. Tens of thousands of California poppies were in prime flower; they covered the entire landscape nearly as far as the eye could see. I made three exposures of the seas of flowers with the 127-mm lens, which is slightly wide angle on the 4" x 5" format. Two of the poppy photos turned out great. They were shot on Ektachrome E-3, which was an excellent film with good color rendition but it lacked long-term color stability. I have sold both images a number of times to magazines and books on wildflowers. Today it hardly seems possible that I took only three exposures, but film was expensive and I was confident that the results would be good.

On that same trip I also photographed, from the safety of my car, a coiled Mojave green rattlesnake near where I planned to take my poppy photographs. It brought home the need to watch one's step when working and not to take anything for granted.

Later that spring I photographed a Jeffrey pine just before sunset along Lightning Ridge Nature Trail in Angeles National Forest. It was my first planned outing to take photos based on impending weather conditions. I arrived just as the storm cleared and found a gnarled old tree laterally snow-encrusted from the blizzard-like conditions at the 7,500-foot level. It was stunning against the clear blue sky. I made two exposures, one with the sky as a background and one with a small cloud behind the top of the tree. The second one was my first really great photograph; it was one of only two good photos processed from 20 sheets of exposed film. Oddly enough, I was so elated with the results that I gave the 18 failures little thought. It was obvious that planning and perseverance could produce great images. I made a number of 20" x 24" prints of the Jeffrey pine tree but was never able to successfully market it to a publisher; however, I still have hope.

After I was discharged from the army in the summer of 1970 I returned to our Iowa farm. In a matter of weeks I had a six-week fall photo trip planned. I left in late September, camping in South Dakota, Wyoming, Colorado, and New Mexico. It was a productive trip although I found it difficult to take good photos while constantly traveling, since the weather is such an important factor for successful photography.

In the subsequent years I have had opportunities to travel to the desert Southwest many times for spring wildflowers, to explore Florida's cypress swamps and photograph its water birds, to hike and explore Hawaii's Na Pali coast trail and to walk through the volcanic fields to the snowy summit of Mauna Loa. In the fall of 1983 I met Bernie Fashingbauer, a naturalist from the Science Museum of Minnesota who was leading a trip to east Africa. The time was right, and I was able to join 13 others on a three-week safari. We saw large game herds on the Serengeti Plains and visited many other national parks in Kenya and Tanzania. This trip had a special significance, for on this journey I met my wife, Linda.

While these trips afar have been an important part of my understanding of the world's ecological processes, they have been only a small part of my total photographic experience. Most of my time has been spent exploring and photographing the Iowa landscape.

During the 1970s I spent a great deal of time photographing birds. It was a most rewarding experience and enabled me to learn about nature from direct observation. Bird photography often requires a great deal of planning and patient observation.

I have always sought out natural areas of high quality; thus it was only a matter of time until I joined the Iowa Natural Heritage Foundation and the Iowa Chapter of The Nature Conservancy. For nearly 20 years, I have eagerly been active in their preservation efforts throughout Iowa. It has been on land owned by these groups, the Department of Natural Resources, and county conservation boards that I have been able to photograph examples of the original Iowa landscape and its vegetation. On at least a few occasions I am sure that my photographs have helped to ensure the protection of important natural areas.

I have always lived on the farm where I was raised and became increasingly concerned that its soil resource was not being adequately cared for. In the spring of 1978 I began farming our 160 acres. It was a good experience, although during the planting and harvesting seasons it took time away from exploration and photography. It was not without merit, however, as I learned about ecological processes while working with the land. On our farm I also began prairie reconstruction, which continues with renewed vigor today. In 1988 I decided to lease out our cultivated land to a neighbor who used good soil conservation practices so I could pursue photography and writing more seriously.

Teaching has always been an important part of my photographic experience. Teaching forces us to evaluate what we believe. I taught a number of adult education classes on nature photography during the 1970s. In 1976 I proposed a natural history photography course for the students in the Department of Animal Ecology at Iowa State University. Working with the students and faculty from 1977 until 1989 was a great experience.

In addition to the semester course Linda and I began to teach weeklong photographic workshops at Iowa Lakeside Laboratory on West Lake Okoboji in northwest Iowa. During these sessions we watched the dawn break and the sun set over the prairies, lakes, and marshes of Dickinson County. In the years that followed we conducted workshops in central, northeast, and southeast Iowa. We made many lifelong friends experiencing nature when conditions for photography were prime.

Prairie plantings on our farm have become an increasingly important part of my photographic record. They are not only easily accessible in every season and weather condition, but they undergo subtle changes as they mature. During the past 140 years Iowa's native prairie landscapes have been reduced by more than 99 percent. For future generations to be able to see what the original Iowa landscape looked like, prairie plant communities will have to be reconstructed. The photographic record of preserved remnants will certainly play a vital role in this process.

I have spent hundreds of early mornings and evenings working frantically before and just after sunrise and at sunset, as well as

*Big bluestem and rock ledges of lichen-covered Sioux quartzite in first
morning sunlight at Gitchie Manitou State Preserve, Lyon County.*

full days, photographing under the soft light of an overcast sky. Each photograph leaves us with an indelible memory of a time and place. While the actual exposure represents only a fraction of a second up to perhaps 20 seconds, the image, when it finally happens, may represent days, weeks, months, or years of planning.

Good photographic equipment is an important part of successful photography, but I have always downplayed having the newest, latest, most sophisticated, and most expensive. My Speed Graphic was used until 1988, when it simply fell apart. I was able to replace it with a used Nagaoka, an ultra-light wooden field camera, for only $200. My lenses include some old and new Schneiders as well as the Ektar lens purchased with the Speed Graphic, which is likely 50 years old but still performs beautifully. When using view cameras, time in the field and good technique are paramount for great results.

Until 1987 I continued to use screw-mounted Pentax 35-mm cameras and lenses, but after meeting Linda, I decided to switch to Canon cameras and lenses so we could share equipment. Our AE-1 cameras have an internal light meter and will work on a shutter priority mode, but they have no other automated features.

As I complete the writing of this book in 1995 advanced technology continues to introduce new films and more sophisticated cameras, and computer-imaging can piece together parts of various photographs to create a situation that did not really occur. Technology offers us many opportunities but does not seem to give us additional time to explore the world around us. We must be ever vigilant if we are to retain a sense of freedom when so few individuals are going our way.

Common & Scientific Names

Anemone, False Rue	*Isopyrum biternatum*
Anemone, Rue	*Anemonella thalictroides*
Ash, Green	*Fraxinus pennsylvanica*
Aspen, Big-tooth	*Populus grandidentata*
Aspen, Quaking	*Populus tremuloides*
Aster, Azure	*Aster azureus*
Aster, Heart-leaved	*Aster cordifolius*
Aster, Smooth	*Aster laevis*
Autumn Olive	*Elaeagnus umbellata*
Avens, Long-plumed Purple	*Geum triflorum*
Badger	*Taxidae taxus*
Basswood, American	*Tilia americana*
Beech, Blue	*Carpinus caroliniana*
Bellflower, Tall	*Campanula americana*
Birch, Paper	*Betula papyrifera*
Birch, River	*Betula nigra*
Birch, Yellow	*Betula alleghaniensis*
Blackbird, Red-winged	*Agelaius phoeniceus*
Blackbird, Yellow-headed	*Xanthocephalus xanthocephalus*
Black-eyed Susan	*Rudbeckia hirta*
Blazing-star, Dotted	*Liatris punctata*
Blazing-star, Rough	*Liatris aspera*
Blazing-star, Tall	*Liatris pycnostachya*
Bloodroot	*Sanguinaria canadensis*
Bluebells, Virginia	*Mertensia virginica*
Bluebird, Eastern	*Sialia sialis*
Bluejoint	*Calamagrostis canadensis*
Bluestem, Big	*Andropogon gerardii*
Bluestem, Little	*Schizachyrium scoparium (Andropogon scoparius)*
Bobolink	*Dolichonyx oryzivorus*
Boxelder	*Acer negundo*
Bufflehead	*Bucephala albeola*

Bullsnake	*Pituophis melanoleucus*
Bulrush	*Scirpus* sp.
Bunchberry	*Cornus canadensis*
Bunting, Indigo	*Passerina cyanea*
Bushclover, Roundheaded	*Lespedeza capitata*
Butterfly, Monarch	*Danaus piexippus*
Cactus, Brittle	*Opuntia fragilis*
Canvasback	*Aythya valisineria*
Cardinal Flower	*Lobelia cardinalis*
Cardinal, Northern	*Cardinalis cardinalis*
Carrion Flower	*Smilas herbacea*
Catbird, Gray	*Dumetella carolinensis*
Cattail, Common	*Typha glauca (Typha latifolia)*
Chat, Yellow-breasted	*Icteria virens*
Cherry, Wild Black	*Prunus serotina*
Chickadee, Black-capped	*Parus atricapillus*
Chuck-will's-widow	*Caprimulgus carolinensis*
Clover, Purple Prairie	*Dalea purpurea (Petalostemon purpureum)*
Clover, White Prairie	*Dalea candida (Petalostemon candidum)*
Clubmoss, Shining	*Lycopodium lucidulum*
Columbine, Wild	*Aquilegia canadensis*
Compass-plant	*Silphium laciniatum*
Coneflower, Gray-headed	*Ratibida pinnata*
Coneflower, Green-headed	*Rudbeckia laciniata*
Coneflower, Pale Purple	*Echinacea pallida*
Coneflower, Prairie (Mexican Hat)	*Ratibida columnifera*
Coneflower, Purple (Southeast)	*Echinacea purpurea*
Coneflower, Purple (Western)	*Echinacea angustifolia*
Coneflower, Thin-leaved	*Rudbeckia triloba*
Cottonwood, Eastern	*Populus deltoides*
Cowbird, Brown-headed	*Molothrus ater*
Crabapple, Prairie	*Malus ioensis*
Creeper, Brown	*Certhia americana*
Creeper, Virginia	*Parthenocissus quinquefolia*
Crow, American	*Corvus brachyrhynchos*
Cuckoo, Yellow-billed	*Coccyzus americanus*
Culver's Root	*Veronicastrum virginicum*
Cup-plant	*Silphium perfoliatum*
Cut-grass, Rice	*Leerzia oryzoides*
Dalea, Nineanther	*Dalea enneandra*
Dandelion, Dwarf	*Kringa virginica*
Dayflower, Erect	*Commelina erecta*
Deer, White-tailed	*Odocoileus virginianus*
Dickcissel	*Spiza americana*

Dogwood, Alternate-leaf	*Cornus alternifolia*
Dogwood, Rough-leaf	*Cornus drummondi*
Dove, Mourning	*Zenaida macroura*
Dragonhead, False	*Physostegia virginiana*
Duck, Ring-necked	*Aythya collaris*
Duck, Wood	*Aix sponsa*
Dutchman's Breeches	*Dicentra cucullaria*
Eagle, Bald	*Haliaeetus leucocephalus*
Eagle, Golden	*Aquila chrysaetos*
Elm, American	*Ulmus americana*
Falcon, Prairie	*Falco mexicanus*
Fern, Bulblet Bladder	*Cystopteris bulbifera*
Fern, Common Polypody	*Polypodium virginianum*
Fern, Creeping Fragile (On soil)	*Cystopteris protrusa*
	(Cystopteris fragilis)
Fern, Fragile (On rock surfaces)	*Cystopteris tenuis (Cystopteris fragilis)*
Fern, Interrupted	*Osmunda claytoniana*
Fern, Lady	*Athyrium filix-femina angustum*
Fern, Maidenhair	*Adiantum pedatum*
Fern, Marginal Shield	*Dryopteris marginalis*
Fern, Ostrich	*Matteuccia struthiopteris pensylvanica*
Fern, Rattlesnake	*Botrychium virginianum*
Fern, Sensitive	*Onoclea sensibilis*
Fern, Smooth Cliff-brake	*Pellaea glabella*
Fern, Spinulose Shield	*Dryopteris carthusiana*
	(Dryopteris spinulosa)
Fern, Walking	*Camptosorus rhizophyllus*
Fesque	*Festuca* sp.
Fir, Balsam	*Abies balsamea*
Flameflower	*Talinum parviflorum*
Flicker, Northern	*Colaptes auratus*
Flycatcher, Great Crested	*Myiarchus crinitus*
Flycatcher, Willow	*Empidonax traillii*
Fox, Red	*Vuples fulva*
Frog, Western Chorus	*Pseudacris triseriata triseriata*
Gamagrass, Eastern	*Tripsacum dactyloides*
Gentian, Bottle	*Gentiana andrewsii*
Gentian, Cream	*Gentiana alba (Gentiana flavida)*
Geranium, Wild	*Geranium maculatum*
Gerardia, Slender	*Agalinis tenuifolia (Gerardia tenuifolia)*
Ginger, Wild	*Asarum canadense*
Goat's Rue	*Tephrosia virginiana*
Golden-eye, Common	*Bucephala clangula*
Goldenrod, Missouri	*Solidago missouriensis*
Goldenrod, Rigid	*Solidago rigida*
Goldfinch, American	*Carduelis tristis*

Goose, Canada	*Branta canadensis*
Goose, Greater White-fronted	*Anser albifrons*
Goose, Snow	*Chen caerulescens*
Gooseberry, Wild	*Ribes missouriense*
Grama, Hairy	*Bouteloua hirsuta*
Grama, Blue	*Bouteloua gracilis*
Grama, Side-oats	*Bouteloua curtipendula*
Grape, Wild	*Vitis* sp.
Grass, Blue-eyed	*Sisyrinchium campestre*
Grass, Buffalo	*Buchloe dactyloides*
Grass, Foxtail	*Setaria* sp.
Grass, Indian	*Sorghastrum nutans*
Grass, June	*Koeleria macrantha*
Grass, Porcupine	*Stipa spartea*
Grass, Slough	*Spartina pectinata*
Grass, Smooth Brome	*Bromus inermis*
Grass, Three-awn	*Aristida tuberculosa*
Grass-of-parnassus	*Parnassia glauca*
Grosbeak, Blue	*Guiraca caerulea*
Grosbeak, Rose-breasted	*Pheucticus ludovicianus*
Grouse, Ruffed	*Bonasa umbellus*
Gull, Ring-billed	*Larus delawarensis*
Hairstreak, Edward's	*Satyyrium edwardii*
Hawk, Ferruginous	*Buteo regalis*
Hawk, Red-tailed	*Buteo jamaicensis*
Hawk, Rough-legged	*Buteo lagopus*
Hawk, Swainson's	*Buteo swainsoni*
Hazelbrush	*Corylus americana*
Hemlock, Water	*Cicuta maculata*
Hepatica, Sharp-lobed	*Hepatica nobilis (Hepatica acutiloba)*
Heron, Great Blue	*Ardea herodias*
Hickory, Shagbark	*Carya ovata*
Honeybee	*Apis mellifera*
Honeysuckle	*Lonicera* sp.
Hummingbird, Ruby-throated	*Archilochus colubris*
Indian Poke	*Veratum viride*
Iris, Blue Flag	*Iris shrevei (Iris virginica)*
Ironwood	*Ostrya virginiana*
Ivy, Poison	*Toxicodendron radicans*
Jack-in-the-pulpit	*Arisaema triphyllum*
Jay, Blue	*Cyanocitta cristata*
Jewelweed	*Impatiens biflora*
Joe Pye-weed, Spotted	*Eupatorium maculatum*
Junco, Dark-eyed	*Junco hyemalis*
Juniper, Common	*Juniperus communis*
Kestrel, American	*Falco sparverius*

Killdeer	*Charadrius vociferus*
Kingbird, Eastern	*Tyrannus tyrannus*
Kingbird, Western	*Tyrannus verticalis*
Kingfisher, Belted	*Ceryle alcyon*
Kinglet, Golden-crowned	*Regulus satrapa*
Kinglet, Ruby-crowned	*Regulus calendula*
Lark, Horned	*Eremophila alpestris*
Leadplant	*Amorpha canescens*
Leek, Wild	*Allium tricoccum*
Lichen, British Soldier	*Cladonia cristatella*
Lichen, Reindeer	*Cladina* sp.
Lily, Wood	*Lilium philadelphicum*
Lobelia, Brook	*Lobelia kalmii*
Loco-weed	*Oxytropis lambertii*
Lovegrass, Sand	*Eragrostis trichodes*
Mallard	*Anas platyrhynchos*
Maple, Black	*Acer nigrum*
Maple, Silver	*Acer saccharinum*
Maple, Sugar	*Acer saccharum*
Marigold, Marsh	*Caltha palustris*
Mayapple	*Podophyllum peltatum*
Meadowfly	*Sympetrum* sp.
Meadowlark, Western	*Sturnella neglecta*
Meadow-rue, Tall	*Thalictrum dioicum*
Meadowsweet	*Spirea alba*
Merganser, Common	*Mergus merganser*
Merrybells	*Uvularia grandiflora*
Milkweed, Butterfly	*Asclepias tuberosa*
Milkweed, Common	*Asclepias syriaca*
Milkweed, Swamp	*Asclepias incarnata*
Mink	*Mustela vison*
Miterwort	*Mitella diphylla*
Monkshood, Northern Wild	*Aconitum noveboracense*
Moonwort, Prairie	*Botrychium campestre*
Moss, *Anomodon*	*Anomodon attenuatus*
Moss, Apple	*Bartramia pomiformis*
Moss, Broom	*Dicranum scoparium*
Moss, Cedar	*Hypnum curvifolium*
Moss, *Grimmia*	*Grimmia laevigata*
Moss, Hair-cap (Prairie)	*Polytrichum commune*
Moss, Hair-cap (Woodland)	*Polytrichum juniperinum*
Moss, *Hedwiga*	*Hedwiga ciliata*
Moss, Sphagnum	*Sphagnum* sp.
Moss, *Tortula*	*Tortula ruralis*
Moss, Tree	*Climacium americanum*
Moss, Wavy Catharinea	*Atrichum undulatum*

Moth, Cecropia	*Hyalophora cecropia*
Moth, Polyphemus	*Antheraea polyphemus*
Mouse, Deer	*Peromyscus maniculatus*
Mouse, Plains Pocket	*Perognathus flavescens*
Mouse, White-footed	*Peromyscus leucopus*
Muskrat	*Ondatra zibethicus*
Nighthawk, Common	*Chordeiles minor*
Ninebark	*Physocarpus opulifolius*
Nuthatch, White-breasted	*Sitta carolinensis*
Oak, Black	*Quercus velutina*
Oak, Bur	*Quercus macrocarpa*
Oak, Chinkapin	*Quercus muhlenbergii*
Oak, Northern Red	*Quercus borealis (Quercus rubra)*
Oak, Pin	*Quercus palustris*
Oak, White	*Quercus alba*
Opossum	*Didelphis virginianus*
Oriole, Northern	*Icterus galbula*
Oriole, Orchard	*Icterus spurius*
Ovenbird	*Seiurus aurocapillus*
Owl, Barred	*Strix varia*
Owl, Burrowing	*Speotyto cunicularia*
Owl, Eastern Screech-	*Otus asio*
Owl, Great Horned	*Bubo virginianus*
Partridge, Gray	*Perdix perdix*
Paspalum	*Paspalum ciliatifolium*
Pasqueflower	*Pulsatilla patens (Anemone patens)*
Pheasant, Ring-necked	*Phasianus colchicus*
Phlox, Cleft	*Phlox bifida*
Phlox, Downy	*Phlox pilosa*
Phlox, Woodland	*Phlox divaricata*
Phoebe, Say's	*Sayornis saya*
Phragmites (Reed)	*Phragmites communis*
Pine, Bristlecone	*Pinus aristata*
Pine, Eastern White	*Pinus strobus*
Pintail, Northern	*Anas acuta*
Plantain, Indian	*Cacalia atriplicifolia*
Plantain, Rattlesnake	*Goodyera pubescens*
Plum, American Wild	*Prunus americana*
Pokeweed	*Phytolacca americana*
Puccoon, Hairy	*Lithospermum caroliniense*
Puccoon, Hoary	*Lithospermum canescens*
Quail, Bobwhite	*Colinus virginianus*
Rabbit, Cottontail	*Sylvilagus floridanus*
Raccoon	*Procyon lotor*
Racerunner, Prairie	*Cnemidophorus sexlineatus viridis*
Racerunner, Six-lined	*Cnemidophorus sexlineatus sexlineatus*

Ragweed, Giant	*Ambrosia trifida*
Ragwort, Golden	*Senecio aureus*
Raspberry, Black	*Rubus occidentalis*
Rattlesnake, Prairie	*Crotalus virdis virdis*
Rattlesnake-masters	*Eryngium yuccifolium*
Redbud	*Cercis canadensis*
Redcedar, Eastern	*Juniperus virginiana*
Redstart, American	*Setophaga ruticilla*
Robin, American	*Turdus migratorius*
Rock Cress, Lyre-leaved	*Arabis lyrata*
Rose, Multiflora	*Rosa multiflora*
Rose, Wild	*Rosa* sp.
Sage, White	*Atemisia ludoviciana*
Sandpiper, Pectoral	*Calidris melanotos*
Sapsucker, Yellow-bellied	*Sphyapicus varius*
Saxifrage, Iowa Golden	*Chrysosplenium iowense*
Scaup, Lesser (Bluebill)	*Aythya affinis*
Serviceberry	*Amelanchier canadensis*
Shooting-star, Jeweled	*Dodecatheon amethystinum*
Shooting-star, Prairie	*Dodecatheon media*
Shoveler, Northern	*Anas clypeata*
Showy Orchis	*Galearis spectabillis (Orchis spectabilis)*
Shrew, Least	*Cryptotis parva*
Shrew, Short-tailed	*Blarina brevicauda*
Skeleton Weed	*Lygodesmia juncea*
Skink, Great Plains	*Eumeces obsoletus*
Skunk, Striped	*Mephitis mephitis*
Skunk Cabbage	*Symplocarpus foetidus*
Smartweed	*Polygonum* sp.
Snake, Eastern Hognose	*Heterdon platyrhinos*
Snake, Garter	*Thamnophis radix haydeni*
Snakeroot, White	*Eupatorium rugosum*
Solomon's Seal, False	*Smilacina racemosa*
Solomon's Seal, Starry False	*Smilacina stellata*
Solomon's Seal, True	*Polygonatum biflorum*
Sparrow, Chipping	*Spizella passerina*
Sparrow, English or House	*Passer domesticus*
Sparrow, Field	*Spizella pusilla*
Sparrow, Fox	*Passerella iliaca*
Sparrow, Grasshopper	*Ammodramus savannarum*
Sparrow, Harris's	*Zonotrichia querula*
Sparrow, Savannah	*Passerculus sandwichensis*
Sparrow, Song	*Melospiza melodia*
Sparrow, Vesper	*Pooecetes gramineus*
Sparrow, White-throated	*Zonotrichia albicollis*
Spiderwort, Prairie	*Tradescantia virginiana*

Spike-moss, Rock	*Selaginella rupestris*
Spruce, Blue	*Picea pungens*
Spruce, Norway	*Picea abies*
Squirrel, Eastern Gray	*Sciurus carolinenesis*
Squirrel, Eastern Fox	*Sciurus niger*
Squirrel, Red	*Tamiasciurus hudsonicus*
Squirrel, Southern Flying	*Glaucomys volans*
Squirrel, Thirteen-lined Ground	*Spermophilus tridecemlineatus*
Squirrel Corn	*Dicentra canadensis*
Starling, European	*Sturnus vulgaris*
Strawberry, Wild	*Fragaria virginiana*
Sumac, Smooth	*Rhus glabra*
Sumac, Staghorn	*Rhus typhina*
Sunflower, Woodland	*Helianthus strumosus*
Swallow, Barn	*Hirundo rustica*
Swallow, Cliff	*Hirundo pyrrhonota*
Swallow, Tree	*Tachycineta bicolor*
Sweet Cicely	*Osmorhiza claytoni*
Sweet-william, Wild (Wet prairie)	*Phlox maculata*
Swift, Chimney	*Chaetura pelagica*
Switchgrass	*Panicum virgatum*
Sycamore, American	*Platanus occidentalis*
Tanager, Scarlet	*Piranga olivacea*
Teal, Blue-winged	*Anas discors*
Thistle, Tall	*Cirsium altissimum*
Thrasher, Brown	*Toxostoma rufum*
Thrush, Wood	*Hylocichla mustelina*
Titmouse, Tufted	*Parus bicolor*
Toad, American	*Bufo americanus americanus*
Toad, Great Plains	*Bufo cognatus*
Toad, Plains Spadefoot	*Scaphiopus bomifrons*
Toad, Woodhouse's	*Bufo woodhousei woodhousei*
Treefrog, Gray	*Hyla versicolor*
Trefoil, Bird's-foot	*Lotus corniculatus*
Trillium, Nodding	*Trillium cernuum*
Trillium, Prairie	*Trillium recurvatum*
Trillium, Snow	*Trillium nivale*
Triodopsis, White-lipped	*Triodopsis albilabris*
Turtle, Illinois Mud	*Kinosternon flavescens flavescens*
Turtle, Ornate Box	*Terrapene ornata ornata*
Twinflower	*Linnaea borealis*
Twinleaf	*Jeffersonia diphylla*
Vervain, Hoary	*Verbena stricta*
Vetch, Crown	*Coronilla varia*
Violet, Bird's-foot	*Viola pedata*
Violet, Common Blue	*Viola papilionacea*

Violet, Downy Yellow	*Viola pubescens*
Violet, Kidney-leaved	*Viola renifolia*
Vireo, Red-eyed	*Vireo olivaceus*
Vole, Meadow	*Microtus pennsylvanicus*
Wahoo, Eastern	*Euonymus atropurpureus*
Walnut, Black	*Juglans nigra*
Warbler, Bay-breasted	*Dendroica castanea*
Warbler, Blackburnian	*Dendroica fusca*
Warbler, Blackpoll	*Dendroica striata*
Warbler, Black-throated Green	*Dendroica nigrescens*
Warbler, Cape May	*Dendroica tigrina*
Warbler, Chestnut-sided	*Dendroica pensylvanica*
Warbler, Magnolia	*Dendrocia magnolia*
Warbler, Mourning	*Oporornis philadelphia*
Warbler, Nashville	*Vermivora ruficapilla*
Warbler, Orange-crowned	*Vermivora celata*
Warbler, Palm	*Dendroica palmarum*
Warbler, Tennessee	*Vermivora peregrina*
Warbler, Yellow	*Dendroica petechia*
Warbler. Yellow-rumped	*Dendroica coronata*
Waterleaf, Virginia	*Hydrophyllum virginianum*
Waxwing, Cedar	*Bombycilla cedrorum*
Weasel, Least	*Mustela nivalis*
Wigeon, American	*Anas ameicana*
Wildrye, Virginia	*Elmus virginicus*
Willow, Black	*Salix nigra*
Willow, Pussy	*Salix discolor*
Woodpecker, Pileated	*Dryocopus pileatus*
Woodpecker, Red-headed	*Melanerpes erythrocephalus*
Wren, Sedge	*Cistothorus platensis*
Yellowthroat, Common	*Geothlypis trichas*
Yew, Canada	*Taxus canadensis*
Yucca	*Yucca glauca*

Technical Information

Description and location. Date. Photo reference number. Camera, lens, film. Lighting. Exposure. Tripods: A sturdy tripod was used unless otherwise noted. I generally used a Bogen 3211 or 3001 tripod with a Bogen 3030 pan/tilt with quick release or a Star D-40.

Eclipse of the moon just after sunset at Cayler Prairie State Preserve, Dickinson County, northwestern Iowa. August 1989. 19-0050. Canon AE-1, Canon 400-mm F-4.5 FD, Canon 1.4x FD extender, Kodachrome 64. 2 sec @ F-8. Two tripods.

The Art of Seeing
Eastern cottonwood (Populus deltoides) *leaf melted into lake ice along the sandy north shore of Storm Lake, Buena Vista County, northwestern Iowa.* March 16, 1989. Mr8922. Nagaoka Field Camera, 210-mm F-5.6 Schneider Symmar-S, Ektachrome-64. Sidelit, just after sunrise. 1 sec @ F-24. Bellows extension: 11 inches.

Winter prairie with Indian grass (Sorghastrum nutans) *and the last remains of a snow cover on the Marietta Sand Prairie State Preserve, Marshall County, central Iowa.* February 18, 1988. Fb8807. Nagaoka Field Camera, 90-mm F-8 Schneider Super-Angulon, Ektachrome-64. Late afternoon sunlight and evening shade. 1 sec @ F-22.

Blue flag iris (Iris shrevei) *and fallen leaves along the edge of a prairie pothole marsh at Anderson Lake, Hamilton County, central Iowa.* November 20, 1991. Nv9116. Nagaoka Field Camera, 210-mm F-5.6 Schneider Symmar-S, Ektachrome-64. Early morning shade. 6 sec @ F-34.

Diversity
Brook lobelia (Lobelia kalmii), *grass-of-parnassus* (Parnassia glauca), *and slender gerardia* (Agalinis tenuifolia) *in a calcareous fen at Silver Lake Fen State Preserve, Dickinson County, northwestern Iowa.* September 1987. 14-0270. Pentax Sp-500, 35-mm F-2 Super Takumar, Kodachrome 25.

Midafternoon, overcast. Exposure not recorded. Hand-held.

Red oak (Quercus borealis), *alternate-leaf dogwood* (Cornus alternifo-lia), *maidenhair fern* (Adiantum pedatum), *and interrupted fern* (Osmunda claytoniana) *on a north-facing slope in sugar maple–basswood forest along Wexford Creek, Allamakee County, northeastern Iowa.* September 11, 1992. Sp9203. Nagaoka Field Camera, 210-mm F-5.6 Schneider Symmar-S, Fujichrome Velvia. Afternoon shade. 1 sec @ F-28.

Bedrock Outcrops

Crustose lichen–covered Precambrian-age Sioux quartzite with circular colonies of Grimmia (Grimmia laevigata) *surrounding* Hedwigia (Hedwigia ciliata), Tortula (Tortula ruralis), *rock spike-moss* (Selaginella rupestris), *and the lichen* Cladonia *at Gitchie Manitou State Preserve, Lyon County, northwestern Iowa.* December 28, 1994. Dc9409. Nagaoka Field Camera, 210-mm F-5.6 Schneider Symmar-S, Fujichrome Velvia. Midmorning, heavy overcast. 15 sec @ F-45.

Walking ferns (Camptosorus rhizophyllus) *on moss- and lichen-covered Pennsylvanian-age sandstone blocks at Wildcat Den State Park, Muscatine County, southeastern Iowa.* October 27, 1978. Ot7824. Speed Graphic, 127-mm F-4.7 Ektar, Daylight Ektachrome 64. Midafternoon, overcast. 1 sec @ F-14.5.

Broom moss (Dicranum scoparium), *cedar moss* (Hypnum curvifolium), *and northern red oak* (Quercus borealis) *leaves on loose Pennsylvanian-age sandstone along the Iowa River at Fallen Rock State Preserve, Hardin County, central Iowa.* November 14, 1977. Nv7706. Speed Graphic, 210-mm F-5.6 Schneider Symmar, Daylight Ektachrome 64. Midafternoon, overcast. 1 sec @ F-22.

Water-sculptured Mississippian-age limestone on Rock Run Creek near the Iowa River in Rock Run Canyon, Hardin County, central Iowa. October 8, 1992. Ot9216. Nagaoka Field Camera, 90-mm F-8 Schneider Super-Angulon, Fujichrome Velvia. Midafternoon, heavy overcast. 20 sec @ F-32.

Old eastern redcedar (Juniperus virginiana) *atop Ordovician-age dolomite palisades north of Bluffton on the Upper Iowa River, Winneshiek County, northeastern Iowa.* August 21, 1975. Ag7516. Speed Graphic, 127-mm F-4.7 Ektar, Daylight Ektachrome 64 (E-3). Midafternoon, overcast. 1 sec @ F-34. Filter CC10B.

Prairie Relicts

Tall blazing-stars (Liatris pycnostachya), *gray-headed coneflowers*

(Ratibida pinnata), *and compass-plants* (Silphium laciniatum) *along a prairie swale in virgin prairie at Doolittle Pothole Prairie, Story County, central Iowa.* July 7, 1990. Jl9011. Nagaoka Field Camera, 90-mm F-8 Schneider Super-Angulon, Fujichrome 50. Sidelit by the sun's first rays. 1/2 sec @ F-32.

Pasqueflowers (Pulsatilla patens) *in dried grasses at Stinson Prairie State Preserve, Kossuth County, north central Iowa.* April 4, 1990. Ap9014. Nagaoka Field Camera, 210-mm F-5.6 Schneider Symmar-S, Fujichrome 50. Afternoon sunlight blocked by a translucent umbrella. 1 sec @ F-34. Bellows extension: 12 inches.

Downy phlox (Phlox pilosa) *and white sage* (Artemisia ludoviciana) *on an abandoned railroad right-of-way, Prairie Creek Wildlife Refuge, western Marshall County, central Iowa.* June 12, 1992. Ju9229. Nagaoka Field Camera, 210-mm F-5.6 Schneider Symmar-S, Fujichrome Velvia. Backlit, early morning sunlight. 2 sec @ F-32.

Culver's root (Veronicastrum virginicum) *and cream gentian* (Gentiana alba) *on the edge of a bur oak* (Quercus macrocarpa) *savanna along the Skunk River, Story County, central Iowa.* October 31, 1994. Ot9437. Nagaoka Field Camera, 90-mm F-8 Schneider Super-Angulon, Lumiere 100. Midmorning, overcast. 1/2 sec @ F-32.

Fruits of American wild plum (Prunus americana) *along a roadside near the Mississippi River, Jackson County, eastern Iowa.* August 11, 1977. Ag7701. Speed Graphic, 210-mm F-5.6 Schneider Symmar, Daylight Ektachrome 64. Midafternoon, overcast. 1 sec @ F-34. Bellows extension: 11 inches.

Great Weather

Compass-plants (Silphium laciniatum) *against cumulus clouds in the evening sky at Prairie Creek Wildlife Refuge, Marshall County, central Iowa.* August 1988. 14-0277. Canon AE-1, Canon Zoom 28-85-mm F-4 FD, Kodachrome 64. Late evening light. Exposure not recorded.

Wall cloud coming in from the west at Prairie Creek Wildlife Refuge, Marshall County, central Iowa. August 1989. 19-0047. Canon AE-1, Canon Zoom 28-85-mm F-4 FD, Kodachrome 64. Midafternoon, very low-level overcast. Exposure not recorded.

Trailing edge of a thunderstorm with mammatus clouds at sunset over Prairie Creek Wildlife Refuge, Marshall County, central Iowa. August 1977. 19-0048. Pentax Sp-500, 35-mm F-2 Super Takumar, Kodachrome 25. Reflected light from the clouds overhead after sunset. Exposure not recorded.

Lightning bolts at the leading edge of an approaching thunderstorm at about 10:00 P.M. in eastern Story County, central Iowa. May 1973. 19-0049. Pentax Spotmatic, 50-mm F-1.4 Super Takumar, Kodachrome II. About 5 min @ F-8.

Tabular hoarfrost at sunset on the open ice of Middle Minerva Creek, Marshall County, central Iowa. January 29, 1993. Jn9319. Nagaoka Field Camera, 90-mm Schneider Super-Angulon F-8, Fujichrome Velvia. Reflected skylight just about sunset. 1 sec @ F-32.

The Bird Habit

Pectoral sandpiper (Calidris melanotos) *in the north pond at Prairie Creek Wildlife Refuge, Marshall County, central Iowa.* October 1988. 04-0160. Canon AE-1, Canon 400-mm F-4.5 FD, Canon 1.4x FD extender, Kodachrome 64. Late evening sunlight just before sunset. Exposure not recorded.

Juvenile barred owl (Strix varia) *at Prairie Creek Wildlife Refuge, Marshall County, central Iowa.* July 1990. 04-0167. Canon AE-1, Canon 400-mm F-4.5 FD, Kodachrome 64. Early morning sun. Exposure not recorded.

American robin (Turdus migratorius) *in early spring migration at Prairie Creek Wildlife Refuge, Marshall County, central Iowa.* April 1988. 04-0159. Canon AE-1, Canon 400-mm F-4.5 FD, Kodachrome 64. Midafternoon, overcast. Exposure not recorded.

Ruby-crowned kinglet (Regulus calendula) *at Prairie Creek Wildlife Refuge, Marshall County, central Iowa.* May 1993. 04-0038. Canon AE-1, Canon 400-mm F-4.5 FD, Canon 15-mm FD extension tube, Kodachrome 64. Late afternoon sunlight and Norman 200-D electronic flash with one head. Exposure not recorded.

Yellow-rumped warbler (Dendroica coronata) *in a black maple* (Acer nigrum) *during spring migration at Prairie Creek Wildlife Refuge, Marshall County, central Iowa.* May 1989. 04-0148. Canon AE-1, Canon 400-mm F-4.5 FD, Kodachrome 64. Midafternoon, overcast. Exposure not recorded.

Iowa's West Coast

Yucca (Yucca glauca), *leadplant* (Amorpha canescens), *nineanther dalea* (Dalea enneandra), *and big bluestem* (Andropogon gerardii) *in Loess Hills prairie at Mt. Talbot State Preserve, Woodbury County, northwestern Iowa.* July 31, 1995. Jl9504. Nagaoka Field Camera, 90-mm F-8 Schneider Super-Angulon, Fujichrome Velvia. Midafternoon, overcast. 1 sec @ F-27.

West side of the Loess Hills formation with yucca (Yucca glauca), *looking south from the top of Murray Hill, Harrison County, western Iowa.* July 1975. 14-0261. Pentax Sp-500, 35-mm F-2 Super Takumar, Kodachrome 25. Midday, hazy sunlight. Exposure not recorded.

Autumn color of smooth sumac (Rhus glabra) *and native prairie grasses in northern Loess Hills landscape at Stevenson Family Preserve, Broken Kettle Grassland (a Nature Conservancy preserve), Plymouth County, western Iowa.* September 1995. 14-0439. Canon AE-1, 50-300-mm F-4.5-FD-L Canon Zoom, Fujichrome Sensia. Late afternoon sunlight just before sunset. Exposure not recorded.

Prairie Marshes

Frost-covered common cattails (Typha glauca) *frozen in clear ice along the edge of Anderson Lake (a prairie pothole marsh), Hamilton County, central Iowa.* November 20, 1991. Nv9113. Nagaoka Field Camera, 210-mm F-5.6 Schneider Symmar-S, Ektachrome 64. Early morning shade. 1 sec @ F-20.

Black willow (Salix nigra) *branches frozen down on the edge of the winter marsh along the edge of Anderson Lake (a prairie pothole marsh), Hamilton County, central Iowa.* January 29, 1992. Jn9208. Nagaoka Field Camera, 210-mm F-5.6 Schneider Symmar-S, Ektachrome 64. Midafternoon, overcast. 1/4 sec @ F-32.

Rime frost on grasses and pussy willows (Salix discolor) *in the south pond at Prairie Creek Wildlife Refuge, western Marshall County, central Iowa.* December 8, 1992. Dc9208. Nagaoka Field Camera, 210-mm F-5.6 Schneider Symmar-S, Ektachrome 64. Midmorning, overcast. 1/15 sec @ F-16.

Canvasback ducks (Aythya valisineria) *during a spring blizzard in the open water of Little Wall Lake, Hamilton County, north central Iowa.* April 1991. 04-0176. Canon AE-1, Canon 400-mm F-4.5 FD, Kodachrome 64. Midafternoon, heavy overcast with blowing snow. Exposure not recorded.

Snow geese (Chen caerulescens) *silhouetted against the sky just after sunrise at Hendrickson Marsh, Story County, central Iowa.* March 1974. 04-0162. Pentax Sp-500, 400-mm F-5 Astro, Kodachrome II. Bright sunrise sky. 1/250 sec @ F-8.

Indian Summer's End

Sugar maple (Acer saccharum) *and an old white oak* (Quercus alba) *in a cold autumn rain at Mossy Glen State Preserve, Clayton County, northeastern Iowa.* October 1977. 21-0064. Pentax Sp-500, 55-mm F-2 Super Takumar,

Kodachrome 25. Midafternoon, overcast with cold rain. Exposure not recorded.

Pennsylvanian-age sandstone covered with the moss Anomodon (Anomodon attenuatus), *marginal shield ferns* (Dryopteris marginalis), *and yellow birches* (Betula alleghaniensis) *along the Iowa River at Fallen Rock State Preserve, Hardin County, central Iowa.* November 14, 1977. Nv7710. Speed Graphic, 210-mm F-5.6 Schneider Symmar, Daylight Ektachrome 64. Midafternoon, overcast. 1 sec @ F-32.

Critters

Juvenile red fox (Vuples fulva) *along a country road in western Marshall County, central Iowa.* June 1992. 07-0171. Canon AE-1, 50-300-mm F-4.5-FD-L Canon Zoom, Kodachrome 64. Late afternoon sunlight just before sunset. Exposure not recorded.

Badger (Taxidae taxus) *atop his mound along a country road in western Marshall County, central Iowa.* August 7, 1976. 07-0174. Pentax Sp-500, 400-mm Astro, Kodachrome 25. Late afternoon sunlight just before sunset. Exposure not recorded.

Thirteen-lined ground squirrel (Spermophilius tridecemlineatus) *with a gray partridge* (Perdix perdix) *egg at Stinson Prairie, Kossuth County, northern Iowa.* April 1990. 07-0175. Canon AE-1, 400-mm F-4.5 FD, Canon 1.4x FD extender, Kodachrome 64. Late afternoon sunlight. Exposure not recorded. (Photo by Linda Kurtz)

Western chorus frog (Pseudacris triseriata triseriata) *from along the Iowa River, Marshall County, central Iowa.* May 1976. 15-0022. Indoor setup, Pentax Sp-500, 135-mm F-3.5 Super Takumar, 43-mm extension tube, Kodachrome 25. Graphlex Strobomatic 500 electronic flash with two heads. Exposure not recorded.

White-lipped triodopsis (Triodopsis albilabris) *in mature sugar maple* (Acer saccharum) *forest in Clayton County, northeastern Iowa.* September 1975. 07-0173. Pentax Sp-500, 135-mm F-3.5 Super Takumar, 27-mm extension tube, Kodachrome II. Graphlex Strobomatic 500 electronic flash with one head. Exposure not recorded.

Cecropia moth (Hyalophora cecropia) *at Prairie Creek Wildlife Refuge, Marshall County, central Iowa.* June 1980. 06-0017. Indoor setup, Pentax Sp-500, 200-mm F-4 Super Takumar, 27-mm extension tube, Kodachrome 25. Graphlex Strobomatic 500 electronic flash with dual heads. 1/60 sec @ F-22.

Native Woodlands

Sugar maples (Acer saccharum) *in mixed deciduous forest at Fort Defiance State Park, Emmet County, northern Iowa.* August 17, 1989. Ag8924. Nagaoka Field Camera, 210-mm F-5.6 Schneider Symmar, Fujichrome 50. Midafternoon, overcast. 1 sec @ F-20.

Serviceberry (Amelanchier canadensis) *in red oak* (Quercus borealis) *woods along the northern shore of Lower Pine Lake at Pine Lake State Park, Hardin County, central Iowa.* April 25, 1992. Ap9215. Nagaoka Field Camera, 210-mm F-5.6 Schneider Symmar-S, Ektachrome 64. Late morning, overcast. 1 sec @ F-32-45.

American sycamore (Platanus occidentalis) *along the floodplain of the Skunk River, Story County, central Iowa.* February 14, 1989. Fb8903. Nagaoka Field Camera, 210-mm F-5.6 Schneider Symmar-S, Ektachrome 64. Midafternoon, moderate overcast. 1 sec @ F-32.

Paper birches (Betula papyrifera), *balsam firs* (Abies balsamea), *and a single eastern wahoo* (Euonymus atropurpureus) *on a steep north-facing slope viewed across the Yellow River at Mountain Maple Hollow (a Nature Conservancy preserve), Allamakee County, northeastern Iowa.* November 21, 1979. Nv7904. Speed Graphic, 210-mm F-5.6 Schneider Symmar, Daylight Ektachrome 64. Midafternoon, heavy overcast. 1/2 sec @ F-16.

Big Kettle

Rough blazing-stars (Liatris aspera) *and goldenrods* (Solidago sp.) *on the slope of the glacial kettle at Freda Haffner Preserve, Dickinson County, northwestern Iowa.* August 1986. 14-0229. Pentax Sp-500, 35-mm F-2 Super Takumar, Kodachrome 25. Late morning sunlight. 1/30 sec @ F-16. Hand-held.

Long-plumed purple avens (Geum triflorum) *in evening light at Cayler Prairie State Preserve, Dickinson County, northwestern Iowa.* August 1992. 14-0217. Canon AE-1, 28-85-mm FD Canon Zoom, Kodachrome 64. Very late evening shade. Exposure not recorded.

Nesting

Female northern flicker (Colaptes auratus) *and juvenile male at their nest cavity in an old dead American elm* (Ulmus americana) *at Prairie Creek Wildlife Refuge, Marshall County, central Iowa.* June 1977. 04-0157. Pentax Sp-500, 135-mm F-3.5 Super Takumar, 16-mm extension tube, Kodachrome II. Midday sunlight and Graphlex Strobomatic 500 electronic flash with two heads. Exposure not recorded. Taken from a tower blind.

Red-eyed vireo (Vireo olivaceus) *with a butterfly chrysalis at its nest on the branch of a silver maple* (Acer saccharinum) *in a farm grove, eastern Story County, central Iowa.* June 1974. 04-0170. Pentax Spotmatic, 135-mm F-3.5 Super Takumar, 16-mm extension tube, Kodachrome II. Graphlex Strobomatic 500 electronic flash with two heads. 1/60 sec @ F-22.

Nest and eggs of a brown thrasher (Toxostoma rufum) *in a gooseberry* (Ribes *sp.*) *at Illinois Grove, western Marshall County, central Iowa.* June 1971. 04-0171. Pentax Spotmatic, 50-mm F-1.4 Super Takumar. Graphlex Strobomatic 500 electronic flash with one head. 1/60 sec @ F-16.

Yellow-billed cuckoo (Coccyzus americanus) *brooding young in an eastern redcedar* (Juniperus virginiana) *tree at Prairie Creek Wildlife Refuge, Marshall County, central Iowa.* September 1978. 04-0168. Pentax Sp-500, 400-mm Astro, 16-mm extension tube, Kodachrome 25. Graphlex Strobomatic 500 electronic flash with two heads. Exposure not recorded. Taken from a ground-level blind.

Male indigo bunting (Passerina cyanea) *and young in a grass-supported nest in an old orchard at Prairie Creek Wildlife Refuge, Marshall County, central Iowa.* June 1971. 04-0158. Pentax Spotmatic, 400-mm Astro, 43-mm extension tube, Kodachrome II. Graphlex Strobomatic 500 electronic flash with one head. 1/60 sec @ F-11-16.

The Prairie Paradox

Cleft phlox (Phlox bifida) *on an alluvial sand prairie along the Cedar River, Linn County, east central Iowa.* May 6, 1989. Ma8901. Nagaoka Field Camera, 210-mm F-5.6 Schneider Symmar-S, Fujichrome 50. Midafternoon, overcast. 1 sec @ F-22.

Rough blazing-stars (Liatris aspera) *and Missouri goldenrod* (Solidago missouriensis) *on the Big Sand Mound, Muscatine County, southeastern Iowa.* August 28, 1993. Ag9320. Nagaoka Field Camera, 90-mm F-8 Schneider Super-Angulon, Fujichrome Velvia. Midafternoon, overcast. 1/2 sec @ F-28.

Sensitive ferns (Onoclea sensibilis) *and meadowsweet* (Spirea alba) *in a sand prairie bog at the Marietta Sand Prairie State Preserve, Marshall County, central Iowa.* July 1, 1978. Jl7802. Speed Graphic, 210-mm F-5.6 Schneider Symmar, Daylight Ektachrome 64. Midafternoon, light overcast. 1/2 sec @ F-38.

Rough blazing-stars (Liatris aspera), *Missouri goldenrod* (Solidago missouriensis), *and paspalum* (Paspalum ciliatifolium) *on the Cedar Hills Sand Prairie State Preserve, Blackhawk County, northeastern Iowa.* August 28,

1974. Ag7444. Speed Graphic, 210-mm F-5.6 Schneider Symmar, Daylight Ektachrome (E-3) 64. Midafternoon, light overcast. 1/4 sec @ F-32. Filter CC10B. Color separation made from a color-corrected Cibachrome print.

Wild roses (Rosa *sp.*), *sand lovegrass* (Eragrostis trichodes), *and white sage* (Artemisia ludoviciana) *in autumn color at the Marietta Sand Prairie State Preserve, Marshall County, central Iowa.* October 1985. 14-0227. Pentax Sp-500, 50-mm F-1.4 Super Takumar, Kodachrome 25. Midafternoon, overcast. Exposure not recorded.

Woodland Wildflowers

Skunk cabbage (Symplocarpus foetidus) *flower and new leaves at Hanging Bog (a Nature Conservancy preserve), Linn County, eastern Iowa.* April 1978. 21-0109. Pentax Sp-500, 55-mm F-2 Super Takumar, Kodachrome II. Midmorning, overcast. Exposure not recorded.

Sharp-lobed hepatica (Hepatica nobilis) *in mixed sugar maple–red oak deciduous forest at Hardin City State Perserve, Hardin County, central Iowa.* April 9, 1994. Ap9403. Nagaoka Field Camera, 210-mm F-5.6 Schneider Symmar-S, Ektachrome 64. Midafternoon, overcast. 1 sec @ F-32. Bellows extension: 12 inches.

Miterwort (Mitella diphylla), *woodland phlox* (Phlox divaricata), *maidenhair fern* (Adiantum pedatum), *and true Solomon's seal* (Polygonatum biflorum) *at Doliver State Park, Webster County, north central Iowa.* May 17, 1993. Ma9324. Nagaoka Field Camera, 90-mm F-8 Schneider Super-Angulon, Fujichrome Velvia. Midafternoon, heavy overcast. 2 sec @ F-22.

Prairie trilliums (Trillium recurvatum) *and creeping fragile ferns* (Cystopteris protrusa) *in mixed deciduous forest Jefferson County, southeastern Iowa.* April 23, 1991. Ap9233. Nagaoka Field Camera, 210-mm F-5.6 Schneider Symmar-S, Fujichrome Velvia. Midafternoon, light overcast. 1 sec @ F-32. Bellows extension: 10 inches.

Jeweled shooting-stars (Dodecatheon amethystinum) *around the base of an old white oak* (Quercus alba) *at Turkey River Mounds State Preserve, Clayton County, northeastern Iowa.* May 1974. 21-0063. Pentax Sp-500, 50-mm F-1.4 Super Takumar, Kodachrome II. Midday, overcast. Exposure not recorded.

The Magic Light

Light from the sunrise streaming in from behind the island through rising steam on Lower Pine Lake, Pine Lake State Park, Hardin County, central Iowa.

October 5, 1988. Ot8806. Nagaoka Field Camera, 210-mm F-5.6 Schneider Symmar, Fujichrome 50. Reflected light from the rising sun and early morning shade. 1/8 sec @ F-32.

Spring green of black walnut trees (Juglans nigra) *in an afternoon thunderstorm at Prairie Creek Wildlife Refuge, Marshall County, central Iowa.* August 1983. 21-0066. Pentax Spotmatic, 50-mm F-1.4 Super Takumar, Kodachrome 25. Strong midafternoon side-lighting. Exposure not recorded.

Northern lights about 5:00 A.M. *at Prairie Creek Wildlife Refuge, Marshall County, central Iowa.* October 1989. 19-0046. Canon AE-1, Canon 50-mm F-1.8, Kodachrome 64. Reflected light from the colored sky only. Several min @ F-1.8.

Meadowfly (Sympetrum *sp.*) *covered with frozen dew at Prairie Creek Wildlife Refuge, Marshall County, central Iowa.* September 1971. 06-0022. Pentax Spotmatic, 50-mm F-1.4 Super Takumar, 20-mm extension tube, Kodachrome II. Early morning shade before sunrise. 1 sec @ F-8-11.

The Photographic Record

Algific (cold air) slope in a cold spring rain at Bluebell Hollow (a Nature Conservancy preserve), Clayton County, northeastern Iowa. May 5, 1991. Ma9120. Nagaoka Field Camera, 90-mm F-8 Schneider Super-Angulon, Fujichrome 50. Cold midafternoon, overcast with moderate rain falling. 1 sec @ F-24.

Edward's hairstreak (Satyyrium edwardii) *on butterfly milkweed* (Asclepias tuberosa) *in a prairie remnant at Talmage Hill, Union County, southwestern Iowa.* August 1980. 06-0018. Pentax Sp-500, 55-mm F-2 Super Takumar, 43-mm extension tube, Kodachrome 25. Midday sunlight. Exposure not recorded.

Big bluestem (Andropogon gerardii) *and rock ledges of lichen-covered Sioux quartzite in first morning sunlight at Gitchie Manitou State Preserve, Lyon County, northwestern Iowa.* December 26, 1991. Dc9117. Nagaoka Field Camera, 90-mm F-8 Schneider Super-Angulon, Fujichrome Velvia. Early morning sunlight. 1 sec @ F-32.

Selected References

Arnett, Ross H., Jr., and Richard L. Jacques, Jr. *Guide to Insects.* Simon & Schuster. 1981.

Behler, John L., and F. Wayne King. *The Audubon Society Field Guide to North American Reptiles and Amphibians.* Alfred A. Knopf. 1979.

Bettis, E.A., III, Jean C. Prior, George R. Hallberg, and Richard L. Handy. "Geology of the Loess Hills Region." *Proceedings of the Iowa Academy of Science* 93(3):78–85. 1986.

Black, Gladys. *Iowa Birdlife.* University of Iowa Press. 1992.

Bonney, Margaret Atherton. "Frontier Settlement and Community Building on Western Iowa's Loess Hills." *Proceedings of the Iowa Academy of Science* 93(3):86–93. 1986.

Boon, Bill, and harlen Groe. *Nature's Heartland: Native Plant Communities of the Great Plains.* Iowa State University Press. 1990.

Bowles, John B. *Distribution and Biogeography of Mammals of Iowa.* Texas Tech Press. 1975.

Brockman, C.F. *Trees of North America: A Field Guide.* Golden Press. 1968.

Burt, William H., and Richard P. Grossenheider. *A Field Guide to the Mammals.* Houghton Mifflin Company. 1964.

Cobb, Boughton. *A Field Guide to the Ferns and Their Related Families.* Houghton Mifflin Company. 1963.

Conant, Roger. *A Field Guide to Reptiles and Amphibians.* Houghton Mifflin Company. 1958.

Cooper, Tom C., Executive Editor. *Iowa's Natural Heritage.* Iowa Natural Heritage Foundation and Iowa Academy of Science. 1982.

Costello, David F. *The Prairie World.* Thomas Y. Crowell Company. 1969.

Crum, Glenn H. "Flora of a Sand Prairie in Black Hawk County, Iowa." *Proceedings of the Iowa Academy of Science* 78:81–87. 1971–1972.

Dinsmore, James J., Thomas Kent, Darwin Koenig, Peter C. Peterson, and Dean M. Roosa. *Iowa Birds.* Iowa State University Press. 1984.

Douglas, Paul. *Prairie Skies.* Voyageur Press. 1990.

Eddy, T. L. "A Vascular Flora of the Swaledale Railroad Prairie in North Central Iowa." *Journal of the Iowa Academy of Science* 95(2):47–54. 1988.

Eilers, Lawrence J., and Dean M. Roosa. *The Vascular Plants of Iowa: An Annotated Checklist and Natural History.* University of Iowa Press. 1994.

Errington, Paul L. *Of Men and Marshes*. Iowa State University Press. 1996.

Fleckenstein, John. *Iowa State Preserves Guide*. Iowa DNR. 1992.

Foster, Steven, and James A. Duke. *A Field Guide to Medical Plants*. Houghton Mifflin Company. 1990.

Halfpenny, James C., and Roy Douglas Ozanne. *Winter, An Ecological Handbook*. Johnson Books. 1989.

Howe, Robert W., Mary J. Huston, William P. Pusateri, Roger H. Laushman, and Wayne E. Schennum. *An Inventory of Significant Natural Areas in Iowa*. Iowa Department of Natural Resources. 1984.

Huffman, D.M., L.H. Tiffany, and G. Knaphus. *Mushrooms and Other Fungi of the Midcontinental United States*. Iowa State University Press. 1989.

Johnson-Groh, Cindy, and Donald R. Farrar. "Flora and Phytogeographical History of Ledges State Park, Boone County, Iowa." *Proceedings of the Iowa Academy of Science* 92(4):137–143. 1985.

Leopold, Aldo. *A Sand County Almanac*. Oxford University Press. 1966.

Lommasson, Robert C. *Nebraska Wildfowers*. University of Nebraska Press. 1973.

Ludlum, David M. *The Audubon Society Field Guide to North American Weather*. Alfred A. Knopf. 1991.

Madson, John. *Where the Sky Began: Land of the Tallgrass Prairie*. Iowa State University Press. 1995.

McGregor, R.L., and T.M. Barkley. *Atlas of the Flora of the Great Plains*. Iowa State University Press. 1977.

Mutel, Cornelia F. *Fragile Giants, A Natural History of the Loess Hills*. University of Iowa Press. 1989.

Peattie, Donald Culross. *A Natural History of Trees of Eastern and Central North America*. Crown Publishers. 1958.

Peterson, R.T., and Margaret McKenny. *A Field Guide to Wildflowers of Northeastern and Northcentral North America*. Houghton Mifflin Company. 1968.

Petrides, George A. *A Field Guide to Trees and Shrubs*. Houghton Mifflin Company. 1986.

Pohl, Richard W. "The Grasses of Iowa." *Iowa State Journal of Science*. Vol. 40, No. 4. May 1966.

Prior, Jean C. "Iowa's Geological Preserves." *Iowa Geology* 9:16–19. 1984.

Prior, Jean C. *Landforms of Iowa*. University of Iowa Press. 1991.

Prior, Jean C. "State Parks: Crossroads with the Geologic Past." *Iowa Geology* 14:9–13. 1989.

Pyle, Robert Michael. *The Audubon Society Field Guide to North American Butterflies*. Alfred A. Knopf. 1981.

Robbins, Chandler S., Bertel Bruun, and Herbert S. Zim. *Birds of North America: A Guide to Field Identification*. Western Publishing. 1966.

Roosa, Dean M., Donald R. Farrar, and Mark Ackelson. "Preserving Natural Diversity in Iowa's Loess Hills: Challenges and

Opportunities." *Proceedings of the Iowa Academy of Science* 93(3):163–165. 1986.

Roosa, Dean M. "Endangered! Twilight of an Era or Dawn of a New Day." *Iowa Conservationist.* July 1978.

Roosa, Dean M. "Iowa Natural Heritage Preservation: History, Present Status, and Future Challenges." *Proceedings of the Iowa Academy of Science* 88(1):43–47. 1981.

Ruhe, Robert V. *Quaternary Landscapes in Iowa.* Iowa State University Press. 1969.

Runkel, Sylvan T., and Dean M. Roosa. *Wildflowers of Iowa Woodlands.* Iowa State University Press. 1987.

Runkel, Sylvan T., and Dean M. Roosa. *Wildflowers of the Tallgrass Prairie: The Upper Midwest.* Iowa State University Press. 1989.

Salisbury, Neil E., and James C. Knox. *Glacial Landforms of the Big Kettle–Locality, Dickinson County, Iowa.* State Preserves Advisory Board. 1969.

Salisbury, Neil E., Ronald Dilamarter, and James C. Knox. *An Eolian Site in Monona County, Iowa.* State Preserves Advisory Board. 1969.

Smith, Daryl D. "Iowa Prairie—An Endangered Ecosystem." *Proceedings of the Iowa Academy of Science* 88(1):7–10. 1981.

Thomson, G.W. "Iowa's Forest Area in 1832: A Reevaluation." *Proceedings of the Iowa Academy of Science* 94(4):116–120. 1987.

Thomson, G.W., and H.G. Hertel. "The Forest Resources of Iowa in 1980." *Proceedings of the Iowa Academy of Science* 88(1):2–6. 1981.

Thoreau, Henry David. *Walden.* Random House. 1965.

Thorne, Robert F. *Relict Nature of the Flora of White Pine Hollow Forest Reserve, Dubuque County, Iowa.* State University of Iowa Studies in Natural History. Vol. 20, No. 6. State University of Iowa. 1964.

Tomanek, G.W. *Pasture and Range Plants.* Phillips Petroleum Company. 1963.

van der Linden, Peter J., and Donald R. Farrar. *Forest and Shade Trees of Iowa, Second Edition.* Iowa State University Press. 1993.

Weaver, J.E. *Prairie Plants and Their Environment.* University of Nebraska Press. 1968.

Index

Publication of *Iowa's Wild Places*
is sponsored by the

IOWA
NATURAL HERITAGE
FOUNDATION
"FOR THOSE WHO FOLLOW"

The Iowa Natural Heritage Foundation is a statewide, member-supported organization dedicated to protecting Iowa's natural resources and "wild places." Its mission is to build partnerships and educate Iowans to protect, preserve and enhance Iowa's natural resources for future generations. This non-profit group is involved in activities ranging from water quality protection to trail establishment and from prairie conservation to wetland restoration.

Established in 1979, the Foundation has helped to permanently protect hundreds of Iowa's wild places, including woodlands, wetlands, prairie, trails, greenways, river corridors and lake shores. While some of these places remain in private ownership, others were purchased or donated for public enjoyment. The Foundation's professional staff is skilled at helping landowners who want to protect the wild places they love.

The foundation is also a leader in regional resource planning, model water quality projects, and conservation education to improve land management and protection.

Members of the Foundation and its project volunteers are truly partners in protecting Iowa's natural heritage "for those who follow." To learn how you can join the Foundation or help protect your favorite wild place, contact:

Iowa Natural Heritage Foundation
Insurance Exchange Building, Suite 444
505 Fifth Avenue
Des Moines, IA 50309-2321
515/288-1846
FAX 515/288-0137